PERSONAL AND FAMILY SURVIVAL

THE HISTORIC COLD-WAR-ERA MANUAL
FOR PREPARING FOR EMERGENCY SHELTER
SURVIVAL AND CIVIL DEFENSE

BY **U.S. OFFICE OF CIVIL DEFENSE**

HISTORIC REFERENCE EDITION

THE DOUBLEBIT HISTORIC PERSONAL PREPAREDNESS LIBRARY
BOOK I

FEATURING
REMASTERED UNABRIDGED HISTORIC MANUALS, TEXTS,
GUIDES, AND SKILLS INSTRUCTION IN PERSONAL SURVIVAL,
EMERGENCY PREPAREDNESS, AND DISASTER RECOVERY

Doublebit Press
Eugene, OR

New content, introduction, and annotations
Copyright © 2020 by Doublebit Press. All rights reserved.

Doublebit Press is an imprint of Eagle Nest Press
www.doublebitpress.com | Eugene, OR, USA

Original content under the public domain. First published in 1966 by the U.S. Office of Civil Defense – U.S. Department of Defense.

This title, along with other Doublebit Press books including the Library of American Outdoors Classics, are available at a volume discount for youth groups, outdoors clubs, or reading groups.

Doublebit Press Legacy Edition ISBNs
Hardcover: 978-1-64389-133-0
Paperback: 978-1-64389-134-7

Disclaimer: Because of its age and historic context, this text could contain content on present-day obsolete methods, outdated skills, inappropriate outdoors activities, outdated medical information, unsafe chemical and mechanical processes, or culturally and racially insensitive content. Doublebit Press, or its employees, authors, and other affiliates, assume no liability for any actions performed by readers or any damages that might be related to information contained in this book. This text has been published for historical study and for personal literary enrichment toward the goal of the preservation of American heritage in outdoors lifestyle, ingenuity, and preparedness.

First Doublebit Press Historic Reference Edition Printing, 2020

Printed in the United States of America when purchased at retail in the USA

INTRODUCTION
To The Doublebit Press Historic Reference Edition

Government-issued civilian and military manuals from every decade contain essential knowledge about personal preparedness, thinking about emergencies, thriving while in the field, and self-sufficiency. Unfortunately, many great government reports, pamphlets, military field manuals, and technical guides from over the years have become less available and harder to find. These have either been rescinded by the armed forces as new information makes old manuals obsolete, or are otherwise forced out of print due to their age. Indeed, many methods and techniques in historic handbooks are obsolete and any action should be approached with care, his does not mean that such manuals are completely worthless by being out of date. In fact, the opposite is true – there is much that we can learn from a historic reading of old handbooks, manuals, and training guides toward personal preparedness and self-sufficiency!

By publishing the Historic Reference Editions of old manuals, field guides, and training books, it is our goal at Doublebit Press to do what we can to preserve and share valuable books, pamphlets, and other works that hold timeless knowledge about preparedness, emergency response, outdoors life, navigation, and survival. Books by U.S. agencies such as the USDA, Forest Service, Office of Civil Defense, Department of Defense, as well as military field books, all provide key insights from a historic reading of their pages. Through remastered reprint editions of preparation-themed handbooks and field manuals, outdoors enthusiasts, bushcrafters, hunters, scouts, campers, survivalists, nature lore experts, and historians can preserve the historic skills and institutional knowledge that was learned through hard lessons at the time these books were written.

This book is an important contribution to preparation and emergency response literature and has important historical and collector value toward preserving the American heritage toward ingenuity and self-reliance. The knowledge it holds is an invaluable reference for practicing skills related to thriving in the outdoors. Its chapters thoroughly discuss some of the essential building blocks of self-sufficiency or survival knowledge that are fundamental but may have been forgotten as equipment gets fancier and technology gets smarter. In short, this book was chosen for Historic Reference Edition printing because much of the basic skills and knowledge it contains could be forgotten or put to the wayside in trade for more modern conveniences and methods.

With technology playing a major role in everyday life, sometimes we need to take a step back in time to find those basic building blocks used for gaining mastery – the things that we have luckily not completely lost and has been recorded in books over the last two centuries. These skills aren't forgotten, they've just been shelved. *It's time to unshelve them once again and reclaim the lost knowledge of self-sufficiency.*

Based on this commitment to preserving our self-sufficiency heritage, we have taken great pride in publishing this book as a complete original unabridged work. We hope it is worthy of both study and collection by outdoors folk in the modern era of self-sufficiency, outdoors, and traditional skills life.

Unlike many other photocopy reproductions of classic books that are common on the market, this Historic Reference Edition does not simply place poor photography of old texts on our pages and use error-prone optical scanning or computer-generated text. We want our work to speak for itself, and reflect the quality demanded by our customers who spend their hard-earned money. With this in mind, each Historic Reference Edition book that has been chosen for publication is carefully remastered from original print books, *with the Doublebit Historic Reference Edition printed and laid out in the exact way that it was presented at its original publication.* We provide a beautiful, memorable experience that is as true to the original text as best as possible, but with the aid of modern technology to make as beautiful a reading experience as possible for books that are typically over a century old. Historians, people looking to prepare for emergencies, and survival enthusiasts alike are sure to appreciate the care to preserve this work!

Because of its age and because it is presented in its original form, the book may contain misspellings, inking errors, and other print blemishes that were common for the age. However, these are exactly the things that we feel give the book its character, which we preserved in this Historic Reference Edition. During digitization, we ensured that each illustration in the text was clean and sharp with the least amount of loss from being copied and digitized as possible. Full-page plate illustrations are presented as they were found, often including the extra blank page that was often behind a plate. For the covers, we use the original cover design to give the book its original feel. We are sure you'll appreciate the fine touches and attention to detail that your Historic Edition has to offer.

For outdoors and military history enthusiasts who demand the best from their equipment, the Doublebit Press Historic Reference Edition reprint of this military manual was made with you in mind. Both important and minor details have equally both been accounted for by our publishing staff, down to the cover, font, layout, and images. It is the goal of Doublebit Historic Reference Edition series to preserve outdoors heritage, but also be cherished as collectible pieces, worthy of collection in any self-sufficiency enthusiast and outdoorsperson's library and that can be passed to future generations.

SM-3-11-A
November 1966

PERSONAL AND FAMILY SURVIVAL

Civil Defense Adult Education Course
Student Manual

DEPARTMENT OF DEFENSE
OFFICE OF CIVIL DEFENSE

INTRODUCTION

THIS manual is for your use in the Civil Defense Adult Education course. It can serve also as a basic home reference for personal preparedness.

The Civil Defense Adult Education Program is managed for the Department of Defense, Office of Civil Defense, by the U.S. Office of Education, Department of Health, Education, and Welfare.

State Departments of Education arrange courses to be held in communities throughout the United States. Instructors are specially trained to teach this course and are furnished the latest information available pertaining to it. Supplementary instruction is adapted, as feasible, to fit the local situation.

This brief manual cannot possibly cover all aspects of the complex matter of United States civil defense. It does, however, provide a general orientation on the subject—enough to give a general understanding of why we have the program, who is responsible for doing what, how civil defense is organized as part of government, and some of the problems involved. Additional information may be obtained if desired from your State or local civil defense agency.

Most importantly, you will come to appreciate the responsibility that you, members of your family, and all other individuals have in being prepared for emergencies. This manual can be a key to your survival. Your knowledge, interest, and actions can help your family and your community meet emergencies, whether they result from an enemy attack or natural disaster.

Federal, State, and local governments are responsible for taking measures to safeguard the public in event of a civil defense emergency. To be successful, these emergency measures must depend upon understanding and action by the public and the steps individuals take for personal preparedness.

Nuclear war can be a threat to anyone. There are no easy, no quick, solutions to defense against it. But there are ways of protecting those millions of people who would survive the direct effects of a nuclear attack.

Shelters which can shield against fallout radiation from nuclear explosions are the principal means of protection. Fallout shelters would enable tens of millions, who otherwise would die from the effects of radiation, to live. Their survival, in healthy condition, would help assure survival of the Nation.

The primary objective of the Office of Civil Defense is to help State and local governments provide the means for saving lives in the event of nuclear attack. The Office of Civil Defense provides leadership in creating a nationwide system of community fallout shelters; in stimulating development of plans for their most effective use; and assisting in development of all the necessary supporting systems, such as warning, direction and control, and shelter management.

 A major portion of a nationwide community fallout shelter system is already in being. The distinctive yellow-and-black community fallout shelter sign is now a familiar identification on buildings and other facilities throughout the United States (see inset). The sign indicates a shelter area that would protect from fallout radiation following nuclear attack. It would be open to the public in the event of such an attack. The nationwide fallout shelter system is ever-increasing as modern low-cost shielding techniques are designed for new and remodeled buildings and eventually become part of the shelter inventory. Ventilation improvements allow for greater capacity in some existing shelter areas.

A shelter space for everyone, readily accessible wherever he may be, is the objective. For the most part, shelters now available make use of the radiation shielding inherent in existing buildings. These were located by the National Fallout Shelter Survey, which began in 1961 and is being conducted by the U. S. Army Corps of Engineers and U. S. Navy Facilities and Engineering Command[1] for the Office of Civil Defense on a continuing basis. This approach has helped keep the cost of the nationwide system low.

Private fallout shelters—home, business, industry—are part of the total shelter resource of the Nation. The Office of Civil Defense encourages development of private shelters and provides technical guidance to help in their development. This includes a program to inform the homeowner of the protection provided by his home if it has a basement, and to advise him how this protection can be improved.

Fallout shelters can protect the immediate survivors of nuclear attack. The U.S. Civil Defense program is dedicated to providing this protection, and in preparing the Nation to cope with disaster.

The crucial factor in recovery from nuclear attack would be the survival of human life—the people who embody the skills, the energy, the capacity for organization, and the ingenuity which is our greatest national asset. Preparations are being made to insure postattack recovery.

---

[1] Formerly "Bureau of Yards and Docks." Redesignation effective May 1, 1966.

TABLE OF CONTENTS

	Page
INTRODUCTION	iii
CHAPTER 1—U. S. Civil Defense	1
CHAPTER 2—Modern Weapons and Radioactive Fallout	13
CHAPTER 3—Public Fallout Shelters	35
CHAPTER 4—Fallout Shelter Occupancy	45
CHAPTER 5—Fallout Protection at Home	53
CHAPTER 6—Community Shelter Planning	81
CHAPTER 7—Preparing for Emergency Operations	87
CHAPTER 8—Emergence from Shelters and Recovery	103
CHAPTER 9—Survival on the Farm	117
APPENDIX —An Outline for Family Emergency Planning	125

CHAPTER 1

U. S. CIVIL DEFENSE

The Need for Civil Defense

Nuclear war is possible. Continuing nuclear weapon development by potential enemies, the Berlin and Cuban crises, and the Southeast Asia situation are dramatic reminders of the uneasy world in which we live. We must keep our defenses strong.

Strategic Objectives

In this age of nuclear weapons, United States continental defense forces have two strategic objectives:

1. To deter a deliberate nuclear attack upon the United States and its allies by maintaining a clear and convincing capability to inflict unacceptable damage on an attacker, even if that attacker were to strike first. The Defense Department terms this capability "Assured Destruction."

2. In the event a nuclear attack should nevertheless occur, to limit damage to our population and industrial capacity. The Defense Department terms this capability "Damage Limitation."

Deterrent Capability

In the two decades since the end of World War II, the United States has built its strategic offensive forces to the point where they are superior in number and quality to those of any other nation. The United States has a deterrent force that includes hundreds of land-based intercontinental ballistic missiles, nuclear-armed missiles in Polaris submarines, and strategic and tactical bombers.

These and other elements of American military power stand as the free world's strongest deterrent to nuclear aggression. By assuring the destruction of an aggressor nation, they make nuclear attack improbable. But they do not make it impossible. And it is this possibility of nuclear attack which necessitates damage-limiting defense forces. A meaningful capability to limit the damage of a determined enemy attack requires an integrated, balanced combination of strategic offensive forces, area defense forces, terminal defense forces, and passive defenses. Such a structure would provide a "defense in depth," with each type of force taking its toll of the incoming weapons, operating like a series of filters or sieves, progressively reducing the destructive potential of the attack. Examples of these forces are Minuteman ICBMs to destroy the second and following waves of an attack before they can leave the ground, the fighter interceptors of the North American Air Defense Command which can cover a large area, and the Nike Hercules surface-to-air missiles. An integral part of the damage-limiting defense structure of the United States is civil defense.

Basic Goal of Civil Defense

The basic goal of civil defense, most simply stated, is to save as many lives as possible in the event of nuclear attack on the United States. This is not to say that civil defense, even in combination with other elements of strategic defense, could prevent widespread destruction in event of attack. Millions of Americans would die, and there is no point in looking away from this harsh reality of nuclear war. But with proper preparations, which are well within the bounds of technical and economic feasibility, millions of other Americans would live to sustain the life of the Nation.

Department of Defense Analysis

While there is no way of predicting with precision the many details in a possible nuclear attack against the United States—how many weapons would be used, what their size or power would be, where they would explode, the exact means of delivering them—there are methods for analyzing the probable hazards involved.

During the past several years, the Department of Defense has conducted intensive probability studies on the effects of various hypothetical large-scale nuclear attacks against the United States. These studies continue.

Among the variable factors considered are diverse combinations of military, urban industrial, and population targets attacked by a variety of air-burst and surface-burst nuclear weapons of different sizes. In addition, other variables considered include how war starts, enemy loss rates due to malfunction of weapons and delivery systems, destruction of incoming weapons by United States military defenses, duration of attack, accuracy of weapons, and wind direction and velocity at different seasons of the year.

The results of these studies indicate that tens of millions of people would survive the blast and heat effects of the weapons, but many of these survivors would be threatened by lethal or disabling fallout radiation. (See fig. 1.)

It is this large group of people—those who would survive the blast and heat effects of a nuclear attack but who would be endangered by radioactive fallout—that the Nation's fallout shelter program is designed to protect.

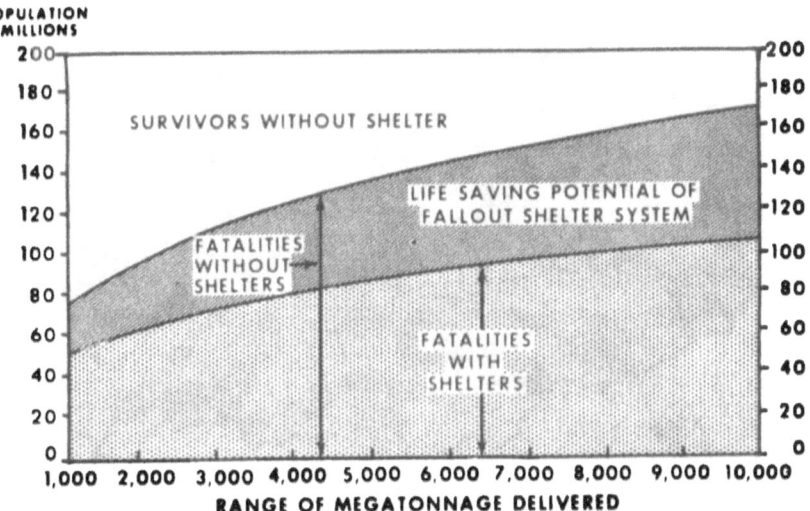

FIGURE 1.—Lifesaving potential of fallout shelter system in attacks against military-urban-industrial targets. In event of attacks against military targets alone, total fatalities would be reduced and lifesaving potential of shelters would be increased. (Source: Composite of Department of Defense damage-assessment studies.)

Hypothetical Attack Results

Figures 2 and 3 show how much of the Nation might be subjected to fallout following hypothetical attacks on a spring day and on a fall day. They show *possible*, not actual, fallout conditions. The attack assumptions were that nuclear weapons were employed, that they totaled in excess of 5,000 megatons[1] in destructive power, and that 65 percent were exploded on or near the ground, generating fallout (see ch. 2). The darkest areas on the maps indicate where it would be necessary to stay in shelter for a week or two. The less dark areas indicate where it would be necessary to stay in shelter from two days to one week. Persons in the light-gray areas on the maps would have to stay in shelter for only a day or two. Approximately 75 percent of the United States would have been covered by radioactive fallout requiring some stay in shelter. The white areas on the maps indicate those areas that did not receive fallout in these hypothetical attacks. Under different attack and meteorological conditions, these areas well might receive fallout, while some of the areas shown here as receiving significant fallout might receive little or none.

Lifesaving Potential of Shelters

A nationwide fallout shelter system is one of a number of options available to strengthen the strategic defense structure of

---

[1] One megaton equals one million tons of TNT.

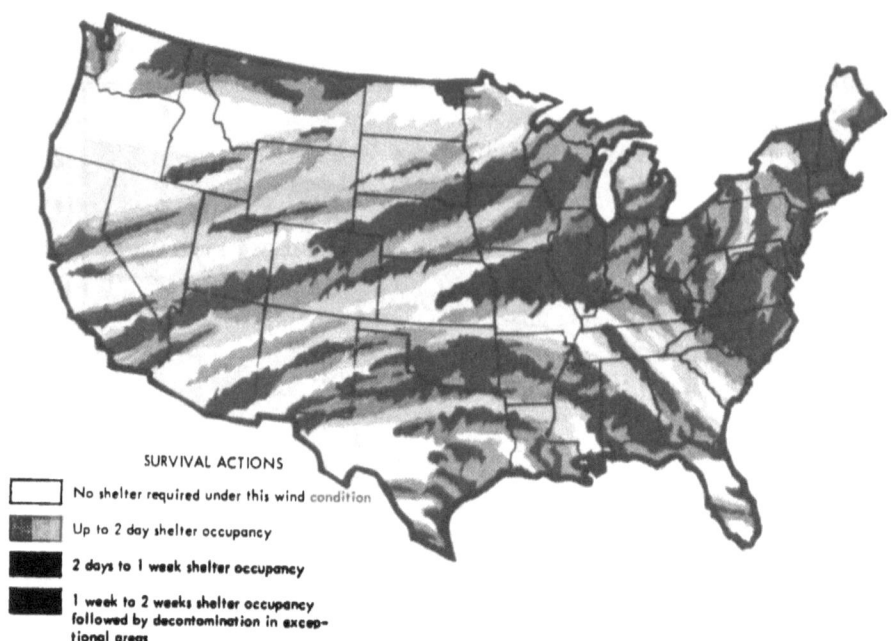

FIGURE 2.—Fallout conditions from a *hypothetical* attack against a wide range of targets: military, industrial, and population (a spring day).

the United States. An antiballistic missile, antisatellite defense, and improved antiaircraft forces are also among these options. Defense Department studies show, however, that a nationwide fallout shelter system has a greater lifesaving potential for the investment involved than any other element of strategic defense, and that it is, in fact, essential to the damage-limiting effectiveness of other strategic defense elements.

The United States is constantly improving its strategic offensive and defensive forces to deter and, if necessary, to meet a nuclear attack. Basic to this improvement is a nationwide fallout shelter system. Developing this system and preparing to make effective use of it in the event of nuclear attack is the central objective of the civil defense program.

Community Shelter Progress

The United States civil defense program is concentrated on planning for the most effective use of the vast community shelter resource already in being across the Nation. The nationwide fallout shelter system exists in many different types of structures all across the land—in office buildings, hotels, libraries, schools, community halls, industrial plants. The dual-purpose capability of structures that are in everyday use is a fortunate circumstance. As of February 1966, the United States public fallout shelter system had a potential for shielding 141½ million persons from the hazards of gamma radiation of nuclear fallout.

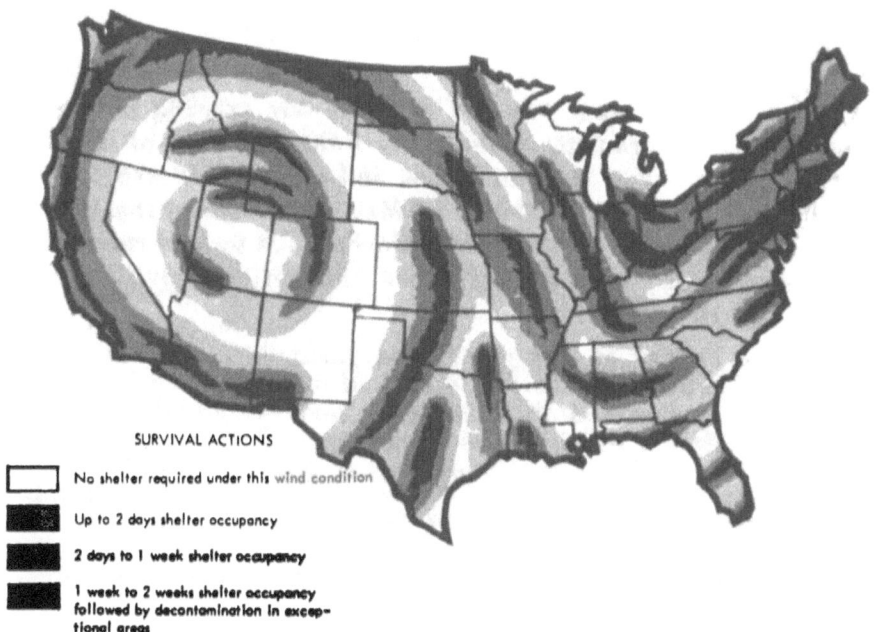

FIGURE 3.—Fallout conditions from a *hypothetical* attack against a wide range of targets: military, industrial, and population (a fall day).

Of this potential, fallout shielding was immediately available, licensed, and/or marked for nearly 92 million people in event of nuclear attack.

Also, as of December 25, 1965, 699 of the 763 cities in which some shelter had been located and 2,237 of the 2,834 counties with some identified shelter were involved in stocking public fallout shelter areas with federally procured austere supplies. These include food, water containers, medical and sanitation kits, and radiation-monitoring instruments. Supplies already in place or immediately accessible to the public shelters in February 1966 were sufficient to sustain more than 38 million persons for at least 2 weeks.

Official Statements

A number of civil and military leaders as well as representatives of the scientific community have expressed their views on civil defense and the fallout shelter program. Following are excerpts from some of these official statements:

In his defense message to the Congress delivered in January 1965, President Johnson emphasized the importance of civil defense as a part of the total national defense posture. The President said—

"It is already clear that without fallout shelter protection for our citizens, all defense weapons lose much of their effectiveness in saving lives. This also appears to be the least expensive way of saving millions of lives, and the one which has clear value even without other systems. We will continue our existing programs and start a program to increase the total inventory of shelters through a survey of private homes and other small structures."

The late President Kennedy, in May 1961, defined the inescapable responsibility of the Federal Government to take reasonable and practicable steps to strengthen the national civil defense capability. He stated that—

"...the history of this planet and particularly the history of the 20th Century is sufficient to remind us of the possibilities of an irrational attack, a miscalculation, and accidental war, or a war of escalation in which the stakes by each side gradually increase to the point of maximum danger which cannot be either foreseen or deterred. It is on this basis that civil defense can be readily justified—as insurance for the civilian population in case of enemy miscalculation. It is insurance we trust will never be needed—but insurance which we would never forgive ourselves for foregoing in the event of catastrophe."

Testifying before the House Armed Services Committee in February 1965, Secretary of Defense Robert S. McNamara made the point that there are—

"...three major programs which constitute our general nuclear war forces: The strategic offensive forces, the continental air and missile defense forces, and civil defense."

Secretary McNamara stressed the need for fallout shelters. In that portion of his testimony relating specifically to civil defense, he said—

"...the major issue in this area concerns the construction of a complete nationwide fallout shelter system. As I noted earlier, such a system would provide the greatest return in terms of lives saved, from any additional funds spent on damage-limiting measures."

He also said—

"...fallout shelters should have the highest priority of any defensive system because they decrease the vulnerability of the population to nuclear contamination under all types of attack."

General Earle G. Wheeler, Chairman, Joint Chiefs of Staff, said to a Special Subcommittee of the Senate Armed Services Committee, in 1963—

"Speaking both for myself as a professional soldier and for the Joint Chiefs of Staff, a fallout-protection-oriented civil defense is clearly a necessary element of the total United States national security effort. Our potential enemies have a clear capability for nuclear warfare, and we cannot discount the possibility that such a war may occur. Prudence and plain common sense dictate that we be prepared for it. An adequate program of civil defense should give our population a reasonable degree of protection as well as increasing the credibility of our military deterrent posture."

The following is from a report, "The Adequacy of Government Research Programs in Non-Military Defense," published by the Advisory Committee on Civil Defense of the National Academy of Sciences (1958):

"Adequate shielding is the only effective means of preventing radiation casualties (in a nuclear attack)." Further on in the report it was stated that, "There is adequate technical knowledge to permit a program of construction of effective shelters to be undertaken immediately."

Concept of Civil Defense as Government in Emergency

Basically, civil defense in the United States is civil government—Federal, State, local—prepared for effective action to limit damage and speed recovery in the event of attack.

The Federal Civil Defense Act of 1950, as amended, states the policy and intent of Congress that "...the responsibility for civil defense shall be vested jointly in the Federal Government and the several States and their political subdivisions."

At the national level, civil defense emphasizes the role of civil government in national defense. This is not the whole of civil defense. Government must also be prepared to act effectively in the wake of many peacetime disasters, and this is particularly required of States and localities where these disasters most frequently strike. But enemy attack would threaten the life of the Nation, and for this reason demands first attention in a nationwide program of civil defense.

The concept of civil defense is a simple one, but one that is sometimes misunderstood. Translated into terms of action, civil defense is the way in which the existing structure of government operating under the officials elected by the people, reacts in time of emergency. It supports and coordinates the use of the best available fallout protection and the public and private emergency service organizations and other resources available to the community for the protection of life and limitation of damage to property.

Confusion concerning this concept exists because civil defense coordination must necessarily be set up, in most cases, as a limited but distinct staff function within the existing structure of government. Civil defense is the planning and emergency action by *all* elements of government, using all resources, public and private, frequently coordinated at the staff level by the civil defense agency, and under the supervision and centralized decision-making of the responsible elected officials.

Civil defense planning involves making special provisions for the emergency ways in which existing government will operate to meet the effects of disaster. Special plans, training, and assignments are required. Special equipment, such as warning devices, must be acquired and kept operational, and special units, such as radiological defense, which may not normally exist in a community, may have to be established to function in emergency.

Two examples may clarify this concept of civil defense. In a west coast city of 200,000, the city manager is also the director of civil defense. He has a full-time deputy who helps him in the planning work and supervises such day-to-day activities as marking and stocking the public fallout shelters. The emergency operating center (EOC) is manned around the clock by the police and fire dispatchers in both normal and emergency periods. All police, fire, public works, parks, and other local government employees have emergency assignments to go with their equipment to specified public shelters. There they automatically come under the supervision of the senior fire official in each shelter complex, or group of shelters, who is assigned as the senior government official for that area. Other employees are trained in shelter management, radiological monitoring, and other emergency skills. Emergency operations are, of course, under the direction of the regular department heads of city government, operating under the supervision and coordination of the city manager-civil defense director just as they normally do.

A Great Lakes city in the over 1 million class has achieved the same result in a somewhat different manner. Here the mayor, with the approval of the council, has appointed a long-time city employee as civil defense director. The mayor and council have delegated to the civil defense director the emergency power to act in their behalf under their policy supervision. The council has also made all city government department heads deputy directors of civil defense. In an emergency, they automatically work under the supervision and coordination of the civil defense director. As in the west coast city, municipal employees have been trained and given emergency assignments.

Basic Federal Civil Defense Authorities

Civil defense activities at the Federal level are carried out under authority established by the Federal Civil Defense Act of 1950, as amended.

On July 20, 1961, the President issued an Executive Order which assigned major civil defense responsibilities to the Secretary of Defense.

To carry out his responsibilities as described in the Executive Order, the Secretary of Defense established the Office of Civil Defense headed by an Assistant Secretary of Defense (Civil Defense), and redelegated to this official the civil defense functions, powers, and authorities assigned to him by the President.

On March 31, 1964, another Department of Defense Directive cancelled the earlier Directive and delegated these civil defense functions to the Secretary of the Army. On the following day, the Secretary of the Army established the Office of Civil Defense, under a Director of Civil Defense, within the Office of the Secretary of the Army, and redelegated his civil defense functions to the Director of Civil Defense.

Office of Civil Defense Organization and Functions

The Office of Civil Defense is part of the Office of the Secretary of the Army. Its national headquarters is in the Pentagon in Washington, D. C. The eight Office of Civil Defense regional offices work directly with the States. The locations of the eight regional offices and the States they serve are shown in Figure 4. It is at this level that direct Federal control of civil defense ends. But the end of the control line is not the end of the responsibility. In civil defense, each level of government does that part of the job which it can do best. The Federal Government is responsible for developing the national program, carrying out work which can best be done nationally, and assisting State and local governments in carrying out their part of the overall national civil defense program which is essential to our total national defense requirements. Assistance is in the form of leadership and guidance, and technical and financial assistance. Examples of national civil defense operations include directing the National Fallout Shelter Survey; development and operation of the national warning system; development, procurement, and distribution of fallout shelter supplies; operation of civil defense training programs; publishing civil defense guidance for State and local governments; developing specialized competence among architects and engineers for incorporation of radiation shielding in buildings through different design techniques; and conducting a coordinated research effort to develop the best methods, materials, and facilities for use by all levels of government in civil defense.

In the civil defense program, the Office of Civil Defense works with the 50 States, Puerto Rico, the Virgin Islands, the Canal Zone, Guam, American Samoa, and the District of Columbia; and through the States, with more than 3,000 counties or parishes, and with more than 17,000 incorporated local governments. The Federal Government matches funds with the States and local governments for personnel and administrative expenses and for the purchase of civil defense supplies and equipment. In addition, the Office of Civil Defense works with the Office of Emergency Planning and some 30 other Federal agencies which have been assigned specific emergency preparedness responsibilities by Presidential Executive Orders.

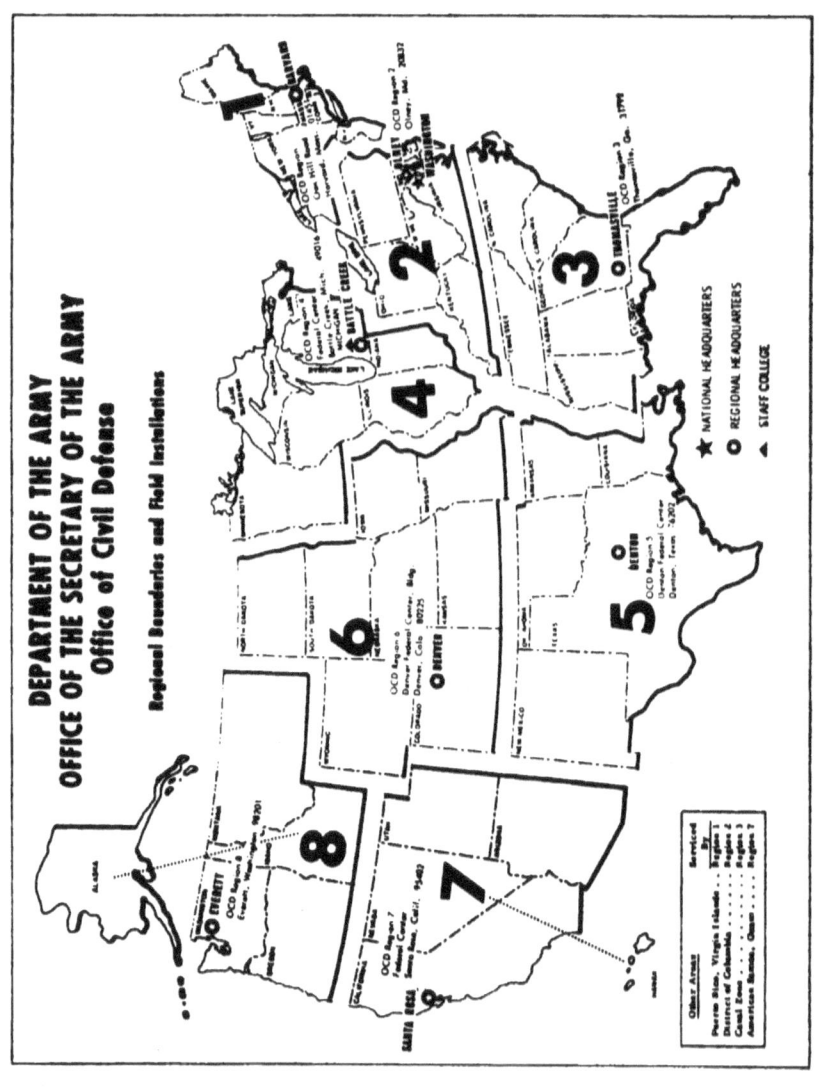

FIGURE 4.—Office of Civil Defense Regions.

State and Local Civil Defense

The basic function of the State or local civil defense director is to act for his chief executive to complete the fallout shelter system and to plan for and coordinate the special actions of other units of government during emergency, whether nuclear attack or natural disaster, under the supervision and authority of the Governor or local elected executive. County commissioners or judges appoint county civil defense directors; and mayors or city managers generally appoint local civil defense directors.

Communities large and small face many problems in protecting their people in emergencies. Many of them have developed civil defense operating plans, and have assigned employees of their government to disaster duties with departments having emergency responsibilities. Some of these employees are given special training for tasks unique to civil defense; for example, radiological monitoring. In many instances, persons outside the regular governmental structure are called upon to augment the emergency forces. Here again, special training often is necessary.

In some geographical areas, mutual-assistance agreements are entered into between and among local political jurisdictions; and by industries—with one another, and with their local governments.

County or area emergency operating plans are often developed in close cooperation with county disaster committees of the U.S. Department of Agriculture, farm cooperatives, granges, and other associations. (See ch. 9, "Survival on the Farm.")

In all communities, the planning and coordinating responsibility for protecting life, alleviating damage, and speeding recovery focuses on the mayor, city manager, or other executive head of local government. He may delegate his authority, but not his responsibility, to a civil defense director whom he appoints. He may assign his civil defense director to assist him in planning for and coordinating the immediate lifesaving actions of government and people in emergency. Actions must be carried out quickly by local government and other forces, in accordance with detailed but flexible local emergency plans. These plans must be supplemented with on-the-spot decisions by appropriate authority to meet the unique problems created by disaster. In peacetime disaster, communities are occasionally isolated from the rest of the world—and local government must "go it alone" at first. This situation would tend to be even more widespread in event of nuclear attack.

CHAPTER 2

MODERN WEAPONS AND RADIOACTIVE FALLOUT

In chapter 1, we looked at the need for a civil defense program in the United States, and at the present organization and responsibilities of the civil defense structure.

To understand the reasons for civil defense, we need to take a look at the weapons of modern warfare.

Although nuclear weapons and the radioactive fallout they produce are rated as the greatest hazard, we must also consider other potential dangers. These include the so-called "conventional weapons," and the chemical (CW) and biological (BW) warfare agents.

The people of the United States must be well aware of the dangers of all of these means of warfare—and how to keep their effects to a minimum if they are ever used.

CONVENTIONAL WEAPONS

Weapons which depend on nonnuclear explosives for their effectiveness are classified as "conventional." These include many of the familiar weapon types used during World War II and the Korean War—such as artillery shells, torpedoes, rockets, and high-explosive and fire bombs. There seems little likelihood that conventional weapons would be used in a strategic attack against the United States.

CHEMICAL AND BIOLOGICAL AGENTS

Studies conducted for the Department of Defense indicate that the threat to the United States posed by chemical and biological agents is relatively less significant than that posed by the nuclear one. Chemical agents are not considered a major strategic threat, as they are effective mainly if used against tactical targets of limited area. Although the possibility of employment of biological agents against U.S. population centers cannot be ruled out, neither a chemical nor biological threat against the continental United States warrants, at this time, the attention and priority given to defense against the effects of nuclear weapons. However, research on methods of detecting, identifying, reporting, analyzing, and defending against biological agents will continue while the potential threat is kept under constant review.

NUCLEAR WEAPONS

Destructive Capabilities

The destructive power of a nuclear weapon is usually described in terms of the total energy it can release in comparison to the number of tons of conventional explosive (TNT) required to release the same amount of energy. Thus, the detonation of a 1-kiloton nuclear weapon releases the same amount of energy as the explosion of 1 thousand tons of TNT; and a 1-megaton nuclear weapon is equivalent in energy release to 1 million tons of TNT.

The results of the World War II conventional bombing attacks on Dresden, Germany; and of the nuclear attack on Hiroshima, Japan, can be compared. In the Dresden raid, a combined British and American operation, February 12-13, 1945, 2,900 tons of conventional bombs were dropped, killing, by German estimates, 120,000 to 150,000 people. At Hiroshima, on August 5, 1945, one bomber dropped one 20-kiloton nuclear bomb. The results were: 70,000 killed, 70,000 injured. The Hiroshima atomic bomb is now considered a weapon of limited power in comparison to current thermonuclear bombs, which can produce explosions equivalent to millions of tons of TNT.

In addition to energy dissipated as blast and shock, a nuclear explosion releases a large proportion of its energy in the form of radiation, creates a flash of light and heat, and a resultant giant fireball. This intense heat can cause skin burns and fires at considerable distances from the point of detonation.

Among all explosives, only nuclear explosions produce nuclear radiations. Initial (immediate) nuclear radiation is defined as the radiation occurring within the first minute after the explosion of a nuclear weapon. Initial radiation effects do not extend beyond the immediate area of severe blast damage. About 90 percent of the total energy released by a nuclear weapon appears in the forms of blast, heat, and initial radiation. The remaining 10 percent of the total energy is released as the residual nuclear radiation which is associated with the radioactive materials resulting from the explosion. These materials and other debris rise with the ascending mushroom cloud, and return to earth as *fallout*.

An enemy might use nuclear weapons in various ways, depending on the results he seeks. He must consider the means available for delivering the weapons, such as aircraft for dropping bombs, or missiles armed with nuclear warheads. He must also consider the effects of various weapon yields and types of burst, in relation to the size of area where destruction will occur, what types of partial or total damage would be inflicted, and how widespread the radioactive fallout would be. A nuclear weapon may be detonated high in the air, at the surface of land or water, or even after the weapon has penetrated below the surface. Descriptions of the three basic types of nuclear bursts—air, surface, and subsurface—are given in figure 5.

TYPES OF BURSTS

AIR BURST

An air burst is defined as one in which the bomb is exploded in the air so high above land or water that the fireball (at maximum brilliance) does not touch the surface. Great blast and heat hazards are produced. The heat wave resulting from the explosion of a one-megaton nuclear weapon can cause moderately severe burns of exposed skin as far as 12 miles from the point of detonation. The warmth may be felt at a distance of 75 miles. Practically no early or close-in fallout is produced.

SURFACE BURST

In a surface burst, the ball of fire touches the ground. Because of its intense heat, large amounts of rock, soil, and other materials will be vaporized and will rise up into the cloud. An important difference between a surface burst and an air burst is that in the surface burst the atomic cloud is much more heavily loaded with this vaporized material; therefore, a surface burst causes much more early radio-active fallout than an air burst.

SUBSURFACE BURST

A subsurface burst is one in which the center of a nuclear explosion occurs under the ground or under water. Underground or underwater shock is produced, and according to the depth at which the explosion occurs, some of the shock will escape to produce air blast. Much of the heat wave and immediate nuclear radiation is absorbed within a short distance by the ground or water. However, large amounts of earth or water near the explosion will be contaminated with radioactive materials.

Consider a one-megaton blast 50 feet underground. The resulting crater would be about 300 feet deep and 1,400 feet across. This means that 10 million tons of rock and soil would be hurled upward from the earth's surface.

FIGURE 5.—Descriptions of the three basic types of nuclear bursts: air, surface, and subsurface.

The radioactive material resulting from an air burst is made up of very small particles. Most of these particles will reach the stratosphere and remain there for long periods of time. When they finally drift down to earth, they are widely distributed and are termed worldwide fallout. Worldwide fallout, because it is widely and thinly distributed and has lost much of its radioactivity through decay by the time it returns to earth, poses a less serious hazard to life than local fallout.

Nuclear detonations at or near the surface of the earth result in the formation of a great quantity of local fallout composed of much larger particles of radioactive debris. This local fallout settles to earth during the first 24 hours. Even so, it can extend in a deadly pattern for hundreds of miles downwind.

Effects of the Explosion

The point on the earth's surface at the center of a nuclear explosion is called ground zero, sometimes abbreviated to GZ. The surrounding land, objects, and persons would be affected in varying ways by heat, blast (shock wave), and radiation, depending primarily on their distance from ground zero, and the size of the weapon. Within a few miles of ground zero, for megaton-size weapons, destruction could be virtually complete, with very few survivors. Moving away from ground zero, the probability of survival would increase, with damage and destruction of structures becoming less severe.

The pattern of effects caused by a nuclear explosion would resemble a series of distorted circles. Terrain features, such as hills and valleys, and large buildings and other surface features would make the patterns irregular. If a weapon is detonated high enough above the surface, no crater is formed, and the blast effects near ground zero are somewhat reduced. Figure 6 illustrates distribution of energy in a typical air burst of a nuclear weapon at an altitude below 100,000 feet. The areas of thermal (heat) effects and blast damage to light structures are materially increased with near-surface air bursts. At higher altitudes, blast and heat effects diminish. The detonation of a nuclear weapon aboard a satellite would produce little damage on the ground.

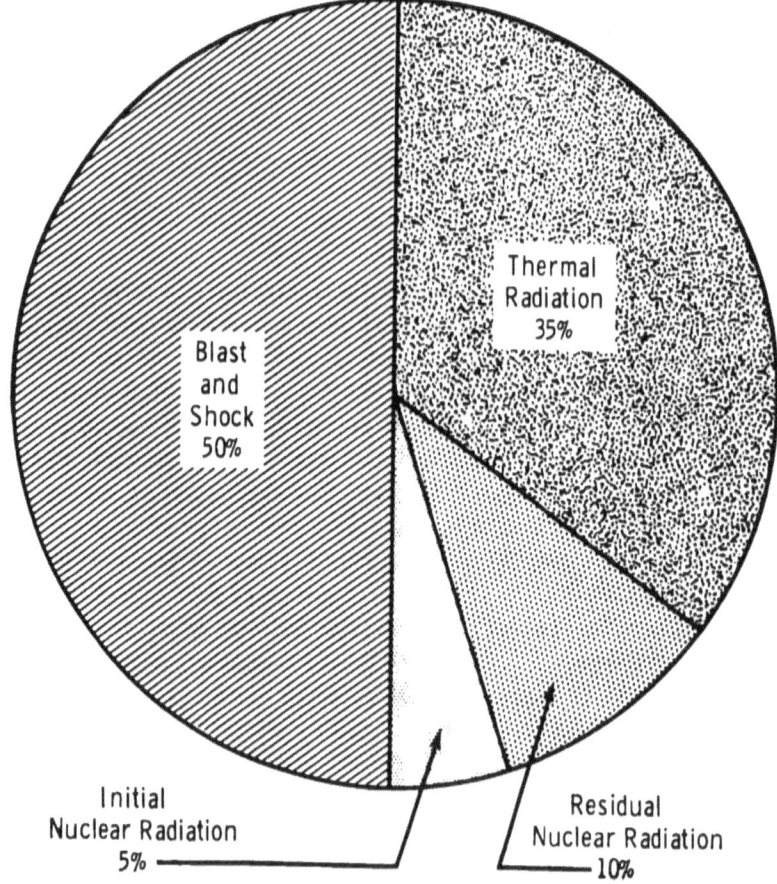

FIGURE 6.—Distribution of energy in typical air burst of a nuclear weapon at an altitude below 100,000 feet.

A large portion of the energy released in the detonation of a nuclear weapon is given off as thermal (heat) radiation. In clear weather, heat can be so intense beyond the range of blast damage that it can ignite papers, fabrics, and thin or dry rotten wood. Fires in these materials may spread to heavier fuels—furniture and other household items, fences, porches, etc.—and then grow to involve entire buildings or groups of buildings.

Individual fires, particularly if there is a wind, might, in some cases, then merge to form larger fires or even conflagrations. These conflagrations are mass fires which, in the presence of a strong surface wind, travel with the wind until they run out of fuel. The famous Chicago fire of 1871 was such a conflagration. In a large congested area with many fires, a "fire storm" might develop. As the individual fires merge, a huge vertically rising column of hot gases and smoke is created. The column is fed by in-blowing winds which become stronger and stronger—fanning the fire to a greater intensity, and eventually causing ignition by thermal radiation instead of flame, just as the weapon does. *The conditions for this type of fire are believed to exist in only certain portions of a few American cities.* Therefore, fire storms are not so serious a threat as the thousands of individual fires and some conflagrations which would be more likely to occur.

The thermal effect of a nuclear attack would be limited greatly by cloud cover, and the spread of fires by barriers composed of areas with little or no burnable material such as open spaces, rivers, wide expressways, and by such weather factors as rainfall and changes in the wind.

The number of fires that might initially occur from a nuclear attack could be significantly reduced by attention to proper maintenance of buildings and to cleanup programs. Their severity could be lessened by extinguishing those individual fires that did occur while they were still small and relatively easy to control.

Effects of an Example 5-Megaton Surface Burst

Some idea of the possible effects of nuclear weapons may be gained from a description of a 5-megaton surface burst. (See fig. 7.) Other weapons of smaller and larger sizes exist; and detonations could be at various altitudes—all of which would change the effects from those in the following example:

A nuclear weapon explodes with a brilliant flash. A quick burst of nuclear and thermal radiation emerges from the fireball. Approximately half of the thermal radiation from a 5-megaton nuclear weapon is released within 4 seconds after the detonation. The remainder is released within one minute. This is followed by a blast (shock) wave which loses much of its damaging force over a distance of about 10 miles. With the blast wave comes a violent wind which can cause additional damage.

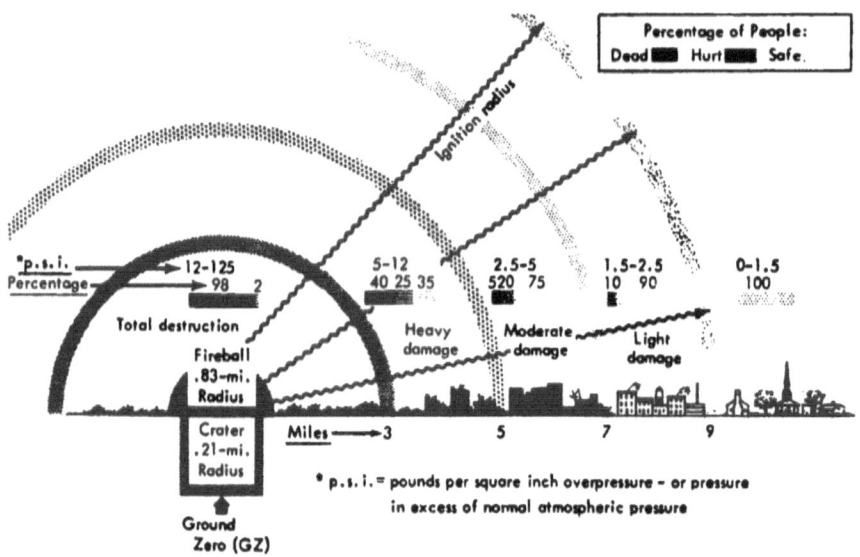

FIGURE 7.—Effects of an example 5-megaton surface nuclear burst.

A 5-megaton burst at ground level would leave a crater about one-half mile wide at the location of the explosion. It would destroy nearly everything within the radius of a mile from ground zero. It would also destroy most buildings 3 miles from the point of explosion, heavily damage steel-frame buildings, and start fires.

The destruction 5 miles away would be less severe, but light structures would be severely damaged or destroyed, and fire and fallout could be significant hazards.

Ten miles away, blast damage to most buildings would be light, but fires could be started indirectly by the blast wave. Gas lines could be ruptured and electric wires knocked down. Flying glass and other debris would also be a major danger.

Somewhat farther away, buildings would remain standing. The fading blast wave would take longer to arrive, but would still shatter many windows. The most acute danger at these greater distances downwind from the explosion would be from early fallout. This might begin to arrive in some areas within 15 minutes to a few hours, depending upon the distance and wind conditions at the time.

The blast, heat, and fire caused by a 5-megaton nuclear explosion could cause widespread destruction out to a distance of about 10 miles. Radioactive fallout could be a great hazard to unprotected persons over an area of thousands of square miles. Although only a small fraction of the total energy expended by a nuclear explosion is released as nuclear radiation, it is this highly important fraction which makes radioactive fallout so serious a danger. What, then, is radioactive fallout?

THE NATURE OF FALLOUT

Description

As stated earlier, in the surface burst of a nuclear weapon, large quantities of earth and other materials are pulverized, melted, vaporized, and mixed with radioactive material. These materials are drawn thousands of feet upward with the rising fireball and the forming mushroom cloud. As the fireball cools, the fission products and other vapors are gradually condensed on the soil and other particles that were sucked up from below while the fireball rises in the air.

The contaminated particles and droplets gradually fall back to earth. The heavier particles fall fairly quickly, near the point of explosion. The lighter particles drift with the upper winds and fall in an irregular pattern that may extend for several hundred miles. This effect is referred to as the "fallout." The particles of fallout, which range in size from coarse to fine sand or table salt, contain highly radioactive material. As previously indicated, the radioactive material resulting from an air burst would not have earth or debris upon which to condense and be carried back to the ground. It would reach the stratosphere and remain there for a long period of time—becoming a part of worldwide fallout.

Time of Fallout Arrival

It takes time for fallout to drop from the nuclear cloud, even close to the burst. The size of a particle is an important factor in determining the length of time required for its return to earth.

The time of fallout arrival at various distances and directions from the point of explosion depends also on the winds and upon the height of the explosion. Layers of air move at different speeds and in varying directions at different heights. Fallout distribution is determined primarily by high-altitude winds that often blow in a quite different direction from the ground-level winds. In a 1954 test, fallout reached a point 160 miles downwind about 8 hours after the explosion and continued to fall for several hours.

Significant amounts of fallout begin to arrive in the immediate vicinity of a blast area soon after an explosion. People some 20 miles away might have an hour to seek protection. At a distance of 100 miles, the fallout may not arrive for 4 hours or more, depending on wind speed. The fallout will continue to cover an increasingly larger area, and may eventually cover several thousand square miles. Some areas might not receive fallout until 24 hours after the explosion, and lighter deposits of fallout might continue for many hours afterwards.

As much as 80 percent of the radioactive material from a land-surface burst of a nuclear weapon may return to the earth as early fallout within the first day. The remaining radioactive material rises high into the sky, is blown around the world by upper-level stratospheric winds, and falls back to earth over a period of months or years.

Area of Severe Fallout

It is impossible to predict with accuracy how large the hazardous downwind area of severe local fallout will be or what shape it will take. Too many conditions can affect it. The area of severe local fallout might stretch 5 miles or more upwind of ground zero, and 150 to 200 or more miles downwind, depending mostly on the strength and direction of the high-altitude winds and the bomb yield. The pattern probably would be irregular in outline, and fallout within the area would not be evenly distributed. There might be local hot spots of radioactivity, as well as other areas with relatively little fallout. These variations could result from differences caused by hills, valleys, lakes, and major rivers; or from wind, rain, and other weather conditions.

In summary, the location and extent of a local fallout area, and the levels of radiation in that area, are determined by:
1. Altitude of the bomb burst.
2. Energy yield and design of the bomb.
3. Size and density of the fallout particles.
4. Atmospheric conditions, such as air currents and the direction and speed of the winds—particularly those up to 80,000 feet.
5. Snow, rain, and hail.
6. Nature of the ground surface.

FALLOUT RADIATION

A brief explanation of the nature of nuclear energy and how it is unlocked from the atom is presented in figure 8.

Kinds of Radiation

Fallout from a nuclear explosion emits beta particles and gamma rays. Beta particles have a maximum range of only 10 to 12 feet in open air (average range 3 to 4 feet). They do not penetrate heavier materials easily. Clothing or other covering can protect the body. But, if enough new fallout remains on exposed skin for some time (hours), the beta particles can cause severe skin damage. This damage would be localized and look somewhat like a severe thermal burn. It might be very painful and discomforting, but no deaths would be expected because of it. Also, if substantial amounts of beta-emitting radioactive material enter the body, some damage may result.

Gamma rays pose the greatest threat, since they have a long range and are extremely penetrating. They may be likened to a kind of invisible light, similar to X-rays, to which all things are partly translucent. Gamma radiation is far more penetrating than beta. Ordinary clothing, which protects against beta, provides essentially no protection against gamma. In a fallout area, the amount of gamma radiation reaching the body can be reduced to acceptable levels by putting enough shielding (mass) between a person and the source of radiation. In general, the denser the material, the lesser of it is required for shielding. If the shielding is thick enough and dense enough, it would cut gamma radiation to such a low level that it would do little harm. This is why buildings with heavy walls or an underground space are more suitable for fallout shelter.

Fallout Cannot Induce Radioactivity

Nuclear radiation from fallout can damage living things, but it cannot make anything radioactive. Thus, if fallout particles are on the body of a person or animal, monitoring instruments may detect nuclear radiation coming from that contamination; but, if the fallout particles are removed, no radiation will be detected because the body itself has not become radioactive.

If radioactive fallout drops into a body of water, the water itself does not become radioactive. After the fallout has settled to the bottom or has been removed by filtration and other normal processing, the water is not radioactive. The same principle applies to water in storage tanks, or to food in cans or other containers. It also applies to air, which is not "poisoned" in any way by radiation passing through it, any more than the air in a doctor's office is poisoned by the X-rays which pass through it when he takes an X-ray of a patient.

HEALTH HAZARDS OF RADIATION

Internal and External Radiation

When large amounts of radiation are absorbed by the body in short periods of time, sickness and death may result. This is why fallout shelters are necessary for protection from fallout radiation.

Radiation damage can result from either ingested or external nuclear radiation. During the early postattack period, external gamma radiation would be the primary hazard. Consumption of heavily contaminated food and water could cause radiation damage, but this hazard would be minor in relation to the external gamma danger.

Foodstuffs contaminated with fallout contain many different radioactive isotopes. Once inside the body, some of these isotopes are concentrated in specific organs, tissues, and bones, and could pose a long-term health hazard. For example, iodine-131 concen-

NUCLEAR ENERGY
All matter is made up of atoms

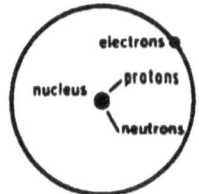

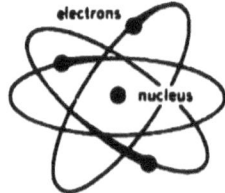

Energy is locked inside the heart, or nucleus, of an atom. The nucleus of every element except ordinary Hydrogen contains neutrons.

Fission. In the process of "fission" (splitting), the atoms of some heavy element, usually Uranium, are broken into and divided. As each nucleus is split, neutrons break free and energy is released. During the process of fission, isotopes are created.

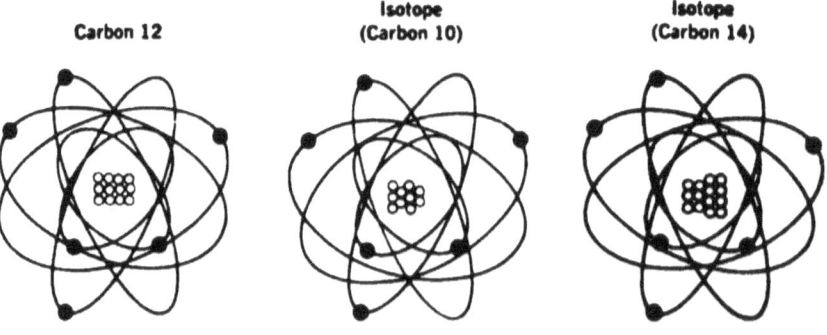

Isotopes are forms chemically like normal elements but atomically different, in that they have a different number of neutrons.

FIGURE 8.—Nuclear energy, and how it is unlocked from the atom.

The free neutrons released by each atom-splitting can, under certain conditions, cause the splitting of others, leading to what is called a *chain reaction*. It is like one match lighting two others, that in turn light others, and so on.

"A-bombs" *(atomic bombs)* are fission weapons. When conditions are just exactly right for a chain reaction, within an extremely small fraction of a second the reaction builds up within a very small space to release enormous amounts of energy. From a relatively small amount of material, there comes a tremendous explosion, many times more violent than is obtained from chemical explosives like dynamite.

FUSION. In nuclear fusion, a pair of light nuclei unite (or fuse) together, to form a nucleus of a heavier atom. An example is the fusion of the hydrogen isotope known as deuterium or "heavy hydrogen." Under suitable conditions, two deuterium nuclei may combine to form the nucleus of a heavier element, helium, with the release of energy. The fusion of all the nuclei present in one pound of deuterium would release roughly the same amount of energy as the explosion of 26,000 tons of TNT.

FIGURE 8.—Nuclear energy, and how it is unlocked from the atom.—*Continued*

trates in the thyroid gland. Strontium-90 behaves much like calcium and is deposited primarily in the bones. Iodine-131 loses its radioactivity relatively rapidly: half of it will decay in about 8 days. It does its damage quickly although the results may not show up for some time. Strontium-90, which decays much more slowly—losing half of its radioactivity in about 28 years—does its damage slowly. Thus, iodine-131 represents a short-term protection problem, while the strontium-90 problem might last years.

Radiation From Natural Sources

Living things are exposed to radiation from natural sources every day. Natural nuclear radiation comes from radioactive rocks and soil; other radiation comes from far out in space. The individual sees nothing and feels nothing, but the radiation damages or destroys some of the body cells. The effects on an individual's health are not serious because very few cells of the body are involved.

Inside the body there are very small amounts of naturally radioactive materials (potassium 40 and carbon 14). Additional amounts are taken in through food, water, and air. Soil and rocks contain potassium 40 and uranium, thorium, and radium. Tiny amounts of these materials are taken into the body with food and water.

Gamma radiation exposure is measured in units called "roentgens" (abbreviated R). The unit is named after W. K. Roentgen, the German physicist who discovered X-rays. A smaller unit often used is a milliroentgen (mR), which is one-thousandth of a roentgen. Radiation intensity, or dose *rate*, is usually measured in roentgens per hour (R/hr).

Small amounts of radiation can be accepted for medical purposes without measurable harm. The average tuberculosis chest X-ray exposes the chest to less than 10 milliroentgens. Even large amounts of radiation can be applied to limited areas of the body without being fatal. Cancer specialists often bombard a cancerous area with massive doses of radiation, destroying more cancer cells than normal cells.

During the average lifetime, every human being is exposed to about 10 roentgens of radiation from natural sources.

Effects of Short-Term Exposure

Few people get sick who have been exposed to 100 roentgens or less. Exposure of the whole body to more than 300 roentgens over a period of a few days will cause sickness and may occasionally cause death. And death would be likely for almost anyone who receives a whole-body exposure of 600 roentgens over a period of a few days. The effects of similar exposures over a period of months or years are still under study. In general, however, it is known that even a fairly large dose of radiation absorbed over months or years is not so dangerous as when absorbed over a few days. In the former case, the body is able to repair much of the cell damage as it occurs.

Individual Exposure Dose

As indicated above, exposure of individuals to radiation should be kept as low as possible. If it should become necessary to leave shelter, the dose rate and the time of exposure would determine the amount of radiation that an individual receives. A simplified method of calculating exposure over a short period is to multiply the intensity by the time of exposure (for example, 3 roentgens per hour times 2 hours equals 6 roentgens). This method is inaccurate over longer periods of time since it does not take into account radioactive decay, which is explained on page 26. The actual dose would be somewhat less than 6 roentgens. Community shelter plans call for trained specialists who would provide guidance on acceptable exposures to radiation under the circumstances.

Radiation Sickness

Persons and animals exposed to large amounts of radiation over short periods of time will develop radiation sickness. Some symptoms are nausea, vomiting, and weakness. They may appear in the first day or so, and then disappear. About a week later other symptoms may appear. These later symptoms may include loss of weight, loss of appetite, bleeding, loss of hair, discolored spots on the skin, paleness, redness, swollen mouth and throat, diarrhea, and general discomfort.

Symptoms of three degrees of radiation sickness are: *Mild*—the especially sensitive person will show some nausea, lack of appetite, and fatigue within a few hours after exposure. He should rest, but can continue normal activities. Recovery will be rapid. *Moderate*—the same symptoms appear, but well within 2 hours of exposure, and more markedly. Vomiting and even prostration may occur. By the third day, recovery may seem complete, but symptoms may recur in the next few days or weeks. *Severe*—again, all the early symptoms show up and may vanish after a few days. But after a week or more, fever, mouth soreness, and diarrhea may appear; gums and mouth ulcerate and bleed; and, in about the third week, the patient's hair may start to fall out. Some people will die. Many others will recover; but recovery may take 7 to 8 weeks.

Symptoms should be treated in this way: General rest. Aspirin for headache. Motion-sickness tablets for nausea. Liquids for diarrhea and vomiting, but not until vomiting has stopped (ideally,

1 tablespoon of table salt to 1 quart of cool water, to be sipped slowly). This solution can be used as a mouthwash for sore mouth.

It is important to remember that many of the symptoms may also appear in people who do not have radiation sickness at all. Symptoms such as nausea, lack of appetite, and fatigue may also be seen in persons subject to extreme anxiety and emotional stress.

Radiation Sickness Not Contagious

Radiation sickness is neither contagious nor infectious; a person cannot "catch it" from others. Persons or animals suffering from radiation sickness can be helped without fear of "catching" it from them. However, a person or animal with symptoms of "radiation sickness" could be suffering from something else, such as a massive infection. It is important therefore to know the history of exposure to radiation, if any. People who have fallout particles on their bodies or clothing probably would not carry enough to endanger other people, but they should clean themselves for their own protection.

RADIOACTIVE DECAY

Radiation intensity from fallout builds up during the time the particles are being deposited. Radiation then decreases with time: that is, the radiation level, as measured in roentgens per hour, drops lower and lower. The decrease is rapid at first, and much slower later on. This falling off of intensity is due to what is termed "radioactive decay." The curve in figure 9 shows the sharp drop in radioactivity in the first 6 to 8 hours following a nuclear explosion, and then a gradual leveling off to a relatively low rate by the end of the first 24 hours. In areas of heavy fallout these rates would still be dangerous. This is why a period of 2 weeks is used for planning shelter occupancy.

During the fission process of a nuclear explosion, isotopes are created. Isotopes are forms of an element which are chemically alike, but atomically different, in that they have a different number of neutrons in their nuclei. Each of the radioactive isotopes formed by a nuclear explosion has a specific half-life or time in which a given quantity of the material will lose one-half of its radioactivity. This ranges from a small fraction of a second to millions of years. The passage of seven half-lives of a radioactive isotope decreases its radioactivity to about 1 percent of its initial level.

The mixture of radioactive isotopes that makes up fallout is so variable and complex as a result of variations in weapon design, soil characteristics, and other factors that it is not possible to calculate the exact decay rate of the total radiation. However, from

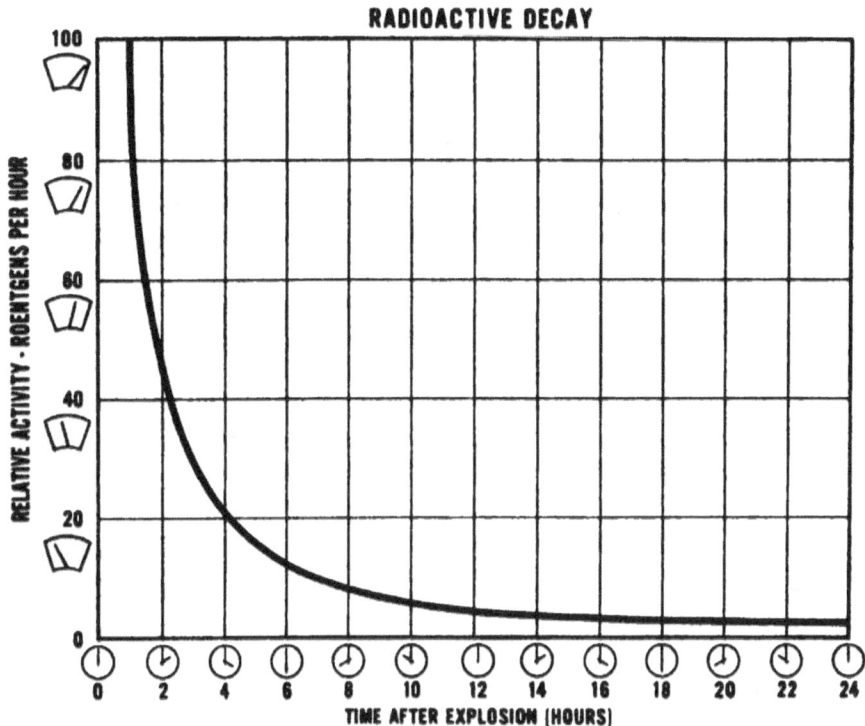

FIGURE 9.—Radioactive decay chart.

experimental measurements, a rough approximation indicated that for each sevenfold increase in time, the radioactivity of the mixture found in fallout drops to about one-tenth of its former value. In general, the radioactivity at 49 hours after the explosion will have dropped to about 10 percent of its level at 7 hours, or 1 percent of what it was 1 hour after the detonation. By the end of about 2 weeks, the radioactivity can be expected to decay by another factor of 10, or to about 0.1 percent of its activity 1 hour after detonation. It must be kept in mind, however, that this approximate time-decay relationship refers to the behavior of the radioactive material; and does not refer to the intensity of gamma radiation at a particular place, unless the radioactive material has been there and is undisturbed during the time being considered.

Decay Cannot Be Speeded Up

It must be emphasized that the radioactivity in fallout cannot be destroyed. Neither boiling nor burning, treatment with chemicals, nor any other action will destroy or neutralize radioactivity. Because of radioactive decay, fallout will become less harmful with the passage of time, but there is no known way to speed up the decay process.

RADIOLOGICAL MONITORING

Fallout particles probably would be visible, especially if potentially lethal contamination levels occur. However, *radiation* given off by the particles cannot be detected by any of the human senses. Radiation cannot be seen, heard, smelled, tasted, or felt: special instruments must be used to detect and measure it.

There are various types of radiation-monitoring instruments. Some of the civil defense radiological monitoring instruments are shown in figure 10. These include dosimeters, which show total radiation exposure of persons; and survey meters, which show the rate of radiation. Radiological monitors are persons specially trained in the use of these instruments.

The dosimeter may be likened to the odometer (mileage indicator) in an automobile, except that it measures total roentgens received (dose) rather than total miles traveled. The ratemeter (or survey meter) may be compared to a speedometer, but it shows roentgens per hour rather than miles per hour.

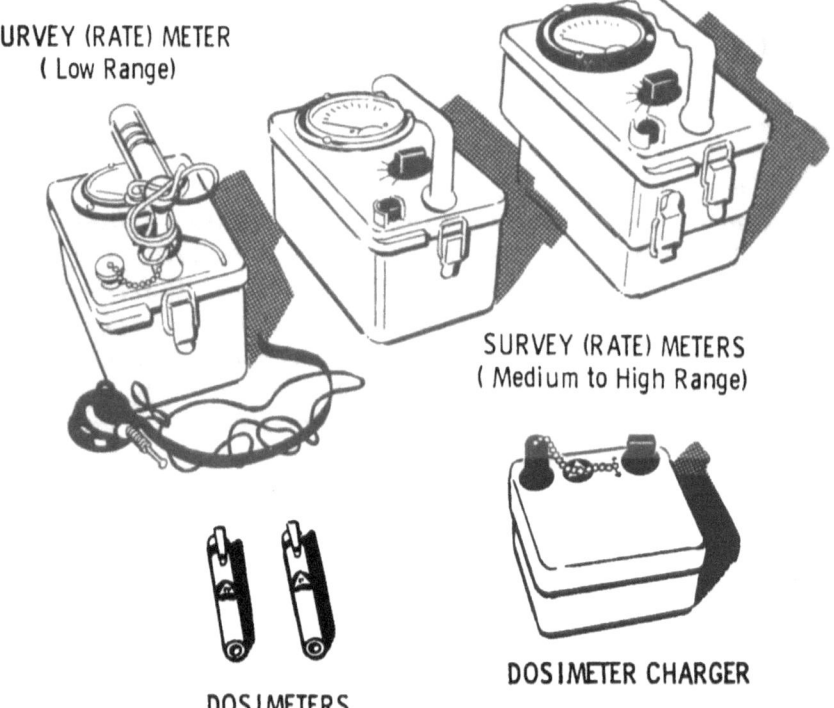

FIGURE 10.—Civil defense radiological monitoring instruments.

Radiological Monitoring and Community Shelters

Kits of instruments are provided by the Federal Government for placement in public fallout shelters. Two or more monitors should be trained for each public shelter. This is a local government responsibility.

Radiation measurements in a shelter could serve as a basis for (a) concentrating the shelter occupants in the best protected areas in the shelter, particularly during the initial period of intense radiation, (b) use of areas adjoining the shelter to alleviate crowding when radiation intensities permit, (c) maintenance of radiation exposure records for shelter occupants, (d) requests to local government officials in the emergency operating center for advice on action in an extreme situation, (e) provision of radiation monitoring information, if requested by the emergency operating center, and (f) provision of fallout situation information to shelter occupants. At the conclusion of the shelter period, monitors and equipment would be used in support of decontamination and other recovery operations.

Area Monitoring

The amount and distribution of radioactivity in a fallout area can be determined accurately only through actual field measurements.

Measurements of radiation levels or intensities can be made from sheltered monitoring stations with remote-reading instruments; or monitors can (after radiation decays somewhat) take quick outside readings. When radiation levels become low enough, mobile monitors can be used. When radiation levels are high or large areas need to be covered quickly, monitoring can be accomplished from airplanes.

Citizens Monitoring Instruments

A citizens radiation-monitoring instrument kit has been commercially developed for sale to the public. The instruments in this kit could be quite useful to those who take shelter in their homes in event of fallout conditions. The kit consists of a ratemeter, dosimeter, and charger. (The ratemeter and dosimeter are similar in appearance.) (See fig. 11.)

Fallout Forecasting

Areas likely to be affected by fallout from a nuclear explosion at any given point can be predicted with fair accuracy, provided the direction and speed of the prevailing winds at each altitude from the earth's surface to high altitudes (80,000 feet) are known. The U.S. Weather Bureau routinely makes frequent observations of winds at all altitudes. After the raw data from these observations are processed by a computer into readily usable form, the information is transmitted by Weather Bureau teletypewriter to Weather Bureau stations and State and local governments for use,

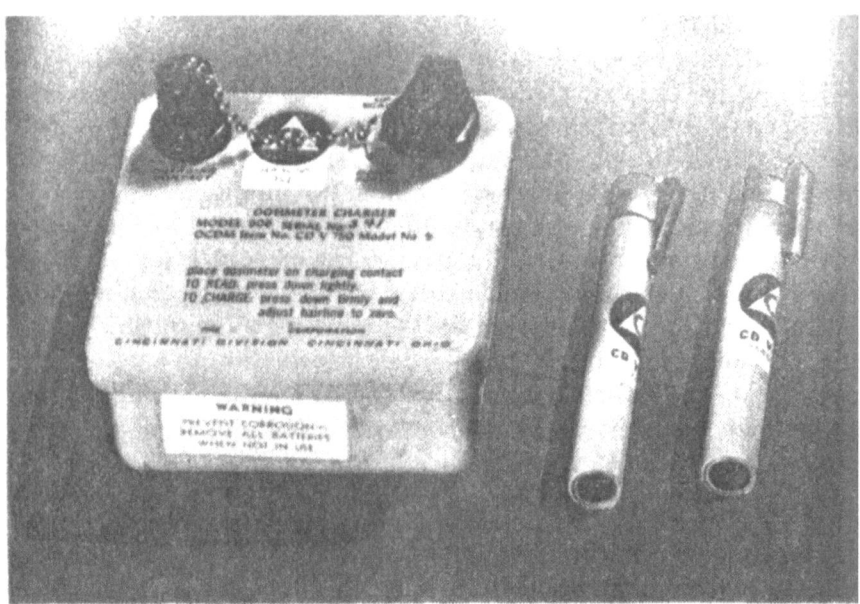

FIGURE 11.—Citizens' radiation-monitoring instrument kit, including ratemeter, dosimeter, and charger.

if necessary, in forecasting the areas of fallout from nuclear detonations, should they occur.

These forecasts can be used to predict *where* fallout is likely to be deposited and approximately when, in terms of time after the detonation, it will arrive there if a nuclear explosion has occurred. The *intensity* of fallout radiation, however, cannot be predicted. Intensity can be determined only after an attack, when measurements would be made with instruments.

Nationwide Radiological Monitoring Network

A nationwide radiological monitoring network has been established, and is being expanded. Each monitoring station has communications to the local emergency operating center, the emergency seat of local government. By early 1966, 56,715 such stations had been established throughout the Nation. In a fallout situation, monitoring stations would furnish frequent reports on the level of radiation at their locations to emergency operating centers, and would serve as bases from which monitors could operate and report during the postattack period when dose rates had decreased to tolerable levels—allowing more extensive surveys to be made.

Local governments are establishing the major portion of the stations in general conformance with State and national plans. Some stations are located in public fallout shelters, while others are in police and fire stations, and State facilities such as State

Police barracks and highway department yards. Several thousand are at field facilities of Federal agencies. The Office of Civil Defense furnishes the required instruments and assists with training programs.

PROTECTIVE MEASURES AGAINST GAMMA RADIATION

Shielding, Distance, Time

Protection from external radiation exposure is a combination of three things: Shielding, distance, and time, defined as—
1. Shielding (shelter).
2. Distance (distance from radiation source), or removal of radioactive materials (decontamination).
3. Time (exposure control) (combination of 1 or 2 above, with time-scheduled exposures). (Radioactive decay is also a function of time.)

In a fallout area, shielding is the most dependable means of protection. Methods of providing shielding are discussed in Chapters 3 and 5. Shelter provides mass between people and the source of radiation. By keeping the fallout outside, shelters also provide some protection by distance. People should remain in shelter until the radiation has decayed to acceptable levels, as determined by specialists.

Special Clothing Offers Little Protection

Fallout gamma radiation would pass through any type of protective clothing that would be practical to wear. Clothing could be useful in keeping fallout particles off the body, but would provide the wearer no protection from the *gamma radiation* given off by the particles. An emergency services worker should wear full outer clothing when in a fallout-contaminated area (after radiation levels decay to specified limits). If contaminated, clothing should be shaken, brushed, or left outside before entering an uncontaminated area.

No Special Antiradiation Medicines

Many experiments have been conducted to develop a special medicine to protect against the effects of radiation. Thus far, there has been some success in laboratory animals; but there seems little likelihood that a pill, or any other type of medicine, will soon be developed that can provide *people* with practical protection from the effects of fallout radiation.

Decontamination

Contamination results from the deposit of fallout particles on the ground, surfaces of structures or other objects, or people, following a nuclear explosion.

Decontamination is the relocation or covering of these fallout particles.

Self Decontamination.—Contamination could be caused by fallout material settling on persons outdoors while fallout was descending or by the person entering a contaminated area after fallout had ceased.

Self-decontamination should be accomplished only after a person first shields himself from the far greater hazard of total radiation in his area. Therefore, if a person is caught out in the open when fallout begins, he should immediately seek cover and *then* remove any contamination from his person by brushing, shaking, or washing before entering shelter, if possible. In most cases, simple wiping, brushing, or washing of hands, face, and clothing would reduce the contamination to tolerable levels.

Decontamination of Food and Water.—It is doubtful that fallout particles that might get inside a building would make food and water dangerous to eat or drink. If food should become contaminated, the fallout particles can usually be removed. Fresh fruits and vegetables can be washed or peeled to remove the outer skin or leaves. Food in cans, covered jars, or other closed containers can be decontaminated by washing or wiping the material off the container. The contents would not be contaminated. Similar cleaning methods appropriate to the type of food involved would, in most cases, be sufficient. Studies indicate that the food and water contamination problem is relatively minor compared to whole-body exposure to radiation from outside sources.

There is a possibility of fallout contamination of surface water supplies such as rivers, lakes, and open reservoirs. Most of the particles of close-in fallout are so heavy that they quickly settle to the bottom. The regular water treatment (coagulation, sedimentation, filtration) of public water systems will remove most of the fallout contamination, since very little of the dangerous fallout material would be dissolved in the water. Water softener systems used in many buildings and homes will remove most of what little fallout may be dissolved in the water in the same manner as they do the chemicals which cause "hard water." Boiling of water is of no value in removing radioactivity. Water from underground sources can be expected to be acceptably free from radiation. Surface water sources could in some instances contain enough radioiodine to be hazardous, especially to children. However, relatively simple and effective means exist to protect against this hazard; and it is short-term. Within a few weeks it would disappear because of dilution and because the radioiodine has a very short half life.

Area Decontamination.—The decontamination of buildings, streets, and equipment needed for priority use shortly after attack might be necessary in some cases before they could be used. Specially trained firemen, engineers, and heavy-equipment operators would undertake this type of decontamination.

Fallout can be relocated by sweeping or through use of high-pressure hoses by fire department or public works personnel.

If you need to decontaminate in your home, common methods of cleaning can be used. Since the fallout particles will only be relocated, care should be exercised to dispose in a safe manner of sweepings, washwater, cleaning rags, and other materials contaminated in the decontamination work. Household decontamination should be undertaken *only* on instructions from local authorities and after it has been determined that radiation levels are low enough to permit activity outside of shelter.

CHAPTER 3

PUBLIC FALLOUT SHELTERS

Fallout shelters are necessary because they provide protection against the widespread danger of fallout. While private shelters will protect some of the people in a community, the major part of the local population will need protection in public shelters. For this reason, American communities are devoting much of their civil defense effort to the licensing, marking, stocking, inspecting, and organizing of public shelters. Such shelters will provide fallout protection for large groups of people if and when the need arises.

THE NATIONAL SHELTER SURVEY

A nationwide survey to locate potential public fallout shelter space in existing structures was started in September 1961. The survey was under the direction of the Office of Civil Defense, assisted by the U.S. Army Corps of Engineers, the U.S. Navy Facilities and Engineering Command,[2] and hundreds of architects and engineers who had been specially trained in fallout shelter analysis. The survey was made possible by procedures which had been developed from more than 5 years of research—procedures whereby a number of complicated calculations on various types of structures could be made rapidly to determine the degree of protection the structures would offer against penetrating gamma radiation.

Much of the survey was completed by 1963; but the survey is a continuing operation to include new building construction and also to take advantage of new information gained through experience in the overall shelter program.

As of mid-1965, specific information had been collected on nearly a half million structures. About a third of these structures contain areas which meet minimum Defense Department requirements for public fallout shelter: (a) a minimum fallout protection factor (PF) of 40;[3] (b) space for at least 50 people at 10 square feet per person; and (c) adequate ventilation.

---
[2] Formerly "Bureau of Yards and Docks." Redesignation effective May 1, 1966.
[3] A fallout protection factor expresses the relationship between the amount of fallout radiation that would be received by an unprotected person compared with the amount he would receive if he were inside shelter. As a general example, a completely unprotected person would be exposed to 40 times more radiation than a person inside a shelter with a fallout protection factor of 40.

35

As of late February 1966, the survey had located more than 161 thousand structures throughout the United States which contain 141½ million fallout shelter spaces. About 60 percent of this shelter resource is in cities of more than 250,000 population; about 40 percent is in smaller cities, towns, and rural areas.

Nearly two-thirds of the surveyed shelter space is in aboveground areas, pointing up an important characteristic of the National Fallout Shelter Program: it aims at dual-purpose emergency use of normally used space; and much of this is found in the inner core areas of multistory buildings.

SHELTER MARKING AND STOCKING

The national survey located existing fallout protection, and computer printouts of this information were sent to State and local governments. Then came the job of preparing to make effective use of this protection as public fallout shelter space. The first step in this process was development of a unique agreement, or "license," involving the building owner, the local government, and the Federal Government.

Under the license, the building owner allows his building to be marked as a public fallout shelter for use in a national emergency, and also to be stocked with austere survival supplies provided by the Federal Government. The building owner receives no payment as a result of this agreement, even though he may be setting aside valuable storage space for the survival supplies. His is a direct personal contribution to the defense of the Nation.

As of February 25, 1966, 89,817 license agreements with building owners had been signed, and black and yellow public fallout shelter signs had been posted on 93,110 facilities containing fallout protection areas for 81,488,000 persons. Meanwhile, the job of stocking this shelter space with essential supplies was well under way.

Studies show that, following nuclear attack, fallout radiation could be a significant immediate danger to human life. Within about 2 weeks, the fallout radiation levels would have decreased so that continuous shelter occupancy would not be required. In most areas of the country, people probably could leave fallout shelter before the end of 2 weeks, at least for brief periods of time. But 2 weeks has been accepted as the basic in-shelter planning criterion.

To meet survival needs of people during shelter occupancy, the civil defense program includes providing austere supplies for all public shelters. These include food, water containers when needed, medical and sanitation items (fig. 12), and radiation-detection instruments. The suitability and adequacy of these supplies have

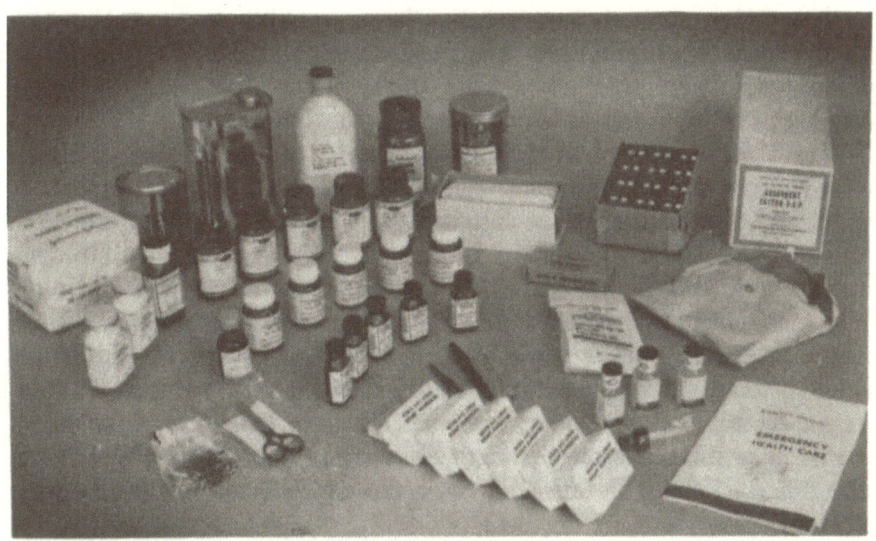

FIGURE 12.—Community shelter stocks include medical kits.

been established in consultation with recognized experts, including the Advisory Committee on Civil Defense of the National Academy of Sciences—National Research Council, the Public Health Service of the Department of Health, Education, and Welfare and the armed services. They have been demonstrated by a series of experiments in which men, women, and children have lived up to 2 weeks in fallout shelters stocked with these supplies.

Since the start of the program, the Office of Civil Defense has procured supplies for 63 million shelter spaces. (A "shelter space" is space for one person.) The average cost of these supplies has been $2.42 per shelter space, broken down as follows:

	Cost per shelter space
Wheat-based biscuit and carbohydrate supplement; 10,000 calories per person	$1.17
Steel water containers with liners; convertible to chemical toilets	0.44
Medical kits for nonprofessional use	0.25
Sanitation kits	0.17
Radiation detection instruments	0.18
Warehousing and transportation costs	0.21
	$2.42

The Office of Civil Defense procures shelter supplies with the specified requirement that they have a minimum shelf-life of 5 years under normal storage conditions. Many items have an indefinite storage life. By February 1966, local governments had stocked public shelters with supplies to sustain more than 38 million people for 2 weeks. But these same shelter areas had a total rated capacity to protect more than 63 million people. The difference between these two figures is largely due to the lack of sufficient storage space for survival supplies in the shelter areas.

The Office of Civil Defense has been working on several ways to decrease the amount of required storage space. These actions should result in lower costs, both to the Government and to building owners who donate storage space for the supplies.

The U.S. Army Corps of Engineers and the U.S. Navy Facilities and Engineering Command, under Office of Civil Defense direction, are now engaged in conducting surveys of buildings containing identified shelter to determine the amount of drinking water "trapped" in the regular plumbing systems of the buildings. The surveys show that there is trapped water in almost every building containing shelter; and that a high percentage of buildings contain trapped water sufficient for essential survival uses during expected shelter occupancy periods. Where insufficient trapped water is available, water-storage containers may be obtained from the Office of Civil Defense through the established shelter supply system.

The shelter survey also has been expanded to collect information on other existing resources in buildings containing shelter space—resources which could reduce the number of stored survival supplies needed in some shelter areas. Included in this appraisal is an analysis of the sewerage capacity of a building. Also, determination is made of the number of water drums needed for secondary use as chemical toilets in shelter areas, and of existing food supplies in the facility which might permit a reduction in the amount of shelter rations needed.

DEVELOPING ADDITIONAL SHELTER SPACE

The basic national survey is expected to locate some 6 million additional shelter spaces every year from new construction and modifications of existing structures. In addition, other actions are being taken to expand the Nation's fallout shelter resource. Emphasis now is on increasing shelter space by making low-cost ventilation improvements, by expanding the survey to cover smaller structures, and by encouraging the incorporation of fallout protection at the design stage of new construction.

Ventilation Improvements

The shelter survey indicates that public shelter space could be considerably increased if conditions of inadequate ventilation were corrected.

Research has developed a method of making significant shelter ventilation improvements at an average cost of about 2 dollars per shelter space added. This low-cost method of making ventilation improvements resulted from the development of a compact, packaged ventilation kit.

The ventilation unit may be operated by a pedal-drive device if electricity is not available. In operation, the kit exhausts stale air from a shelter area through a plastic duct, causing replacement air to be pulled into the shelter through all available openings, such as interior doorways and stairwells.

Smaller Structures Survey

Under criteria established for the National Shelter Survey, only those structures obviously capable of accommodating 50 or more persons were considered. The Office of Civil Defense estimates there are also more than 900 thousand smaller structures, exclusive of 1, 2, and 3-family homes—half of which contain fallout shelter space meeting Office of Civil Defense criteria. It is further estimated that there are 16 million shelter spaces in these buildings, and that by 1970 new construction will raise this to 20 million shelter spaces. The Office of Civil Defense intends to have these buildings which are located in shelter-deficit areas surveyed by the Corps of Engineers and the Facilities Engineering Command.

In addition, many 1, 2, and 3-family homes have a significant amount of fallout radiation protection. With the cooperation of the Bureau of the Census, the Office of Civil Defense is conducting test surveys to determine whether a questionnaire-computer process is a sound method to use to compile information on home fallout protection on a nationwide basis. To date, sample surveys indicate that 76 percent of the houses that have basements have a protection factor of at least 20 in the best protected corner of the basement. The sample surveys also indicate that 10 percent of all homes with basements afford a protection factor of 40 or better.

The "small structures survey" methods of locating fallout protection could be particularly important in suburban and rural areas where more shelter is needed. Meanwhile, the Office of Civil Defense continues to work closely with the U.S. Department of Agriculture, which conducts an extensive information program on rural civil defense, with emphasis on developing protection from radioactive fallout.

Professional Design Development

More than 10,000 architects and engineers have completed courses sponsored by the Office of Civil Defense in fallout shelter analysis, and have been certified by the Department of Defense as Fallout Shelter Analysts. These courses are continuing. The Office of Civil Defense regularly sends information to these specially trained professionals.

Office of Civil Defense technical publications available to architects and engineers and to school boards, business executives, and others planning construction of buildings describe how architects have taken full advantage of "slanting" techniques to provide fallout protection in normally used buildings.

"Slanting" is defined as use of design techniques which incorporate fallout protection in a building—without adversely affecting the normal function, appearance, or cost of the building. In applying "slanting" when designing a building, an architect considers a number of questions. For example:

—Could window areas be reduced or could sills be raised to reduce exposure to radiation?

—Is the structure located so that maximum advantage is taken of mutual shielding from adjacent structures?

—Has consideration been given to use of retaining walls, planters, overhangs, or grading a slope away from the structure to minimize the effect of radiation from the ground?

—Is it possible to depress the ground floor partially or completely below grade to reduce the effect of radiation from the ground?

—Have entrances and exits been located to maximize the protection afforded by baffles, or do they permit direct entry of ground radiation?

—Can stairwells be positioned so that they provide additional shielding at the ends of corridors and hallways?

—Have interior partitions been placed to block radiation?

—Have dense, solid walls been used advantageously, and have hollow walls been filled with low-cost materials such as sand where feasible?

—Has maximum advantage been taken in the arrangement of building elements to provide a protected core area which could be used for shelter?

The above questions reflect some of the many techniques which can result in the design of no-cost or low-cost fallout protection.

PUBLIC FALLOUT SHELTER CONSIDERATIONS

For most of the population, public shelters provide the best answer to fallout protection. People away from home at the time of an attack need to have shelter immediately available.

As a member of a group, a person may better face the problems of shelter living. People could expect to find more special skills— for example, medical skills— represented within a group of many persons than with a small family unit. A large number of people could also share any necessary radiation exposure; for example, in leaving a shelter area for a short time. This would minimize the exposure to each person.

Public shelters may consist of shielded space in the inner cores of buildings (fig. 13), in a basement, in underground chambers, in subways, or in other suitable space. The exact nature of the space or design may vary greatly.

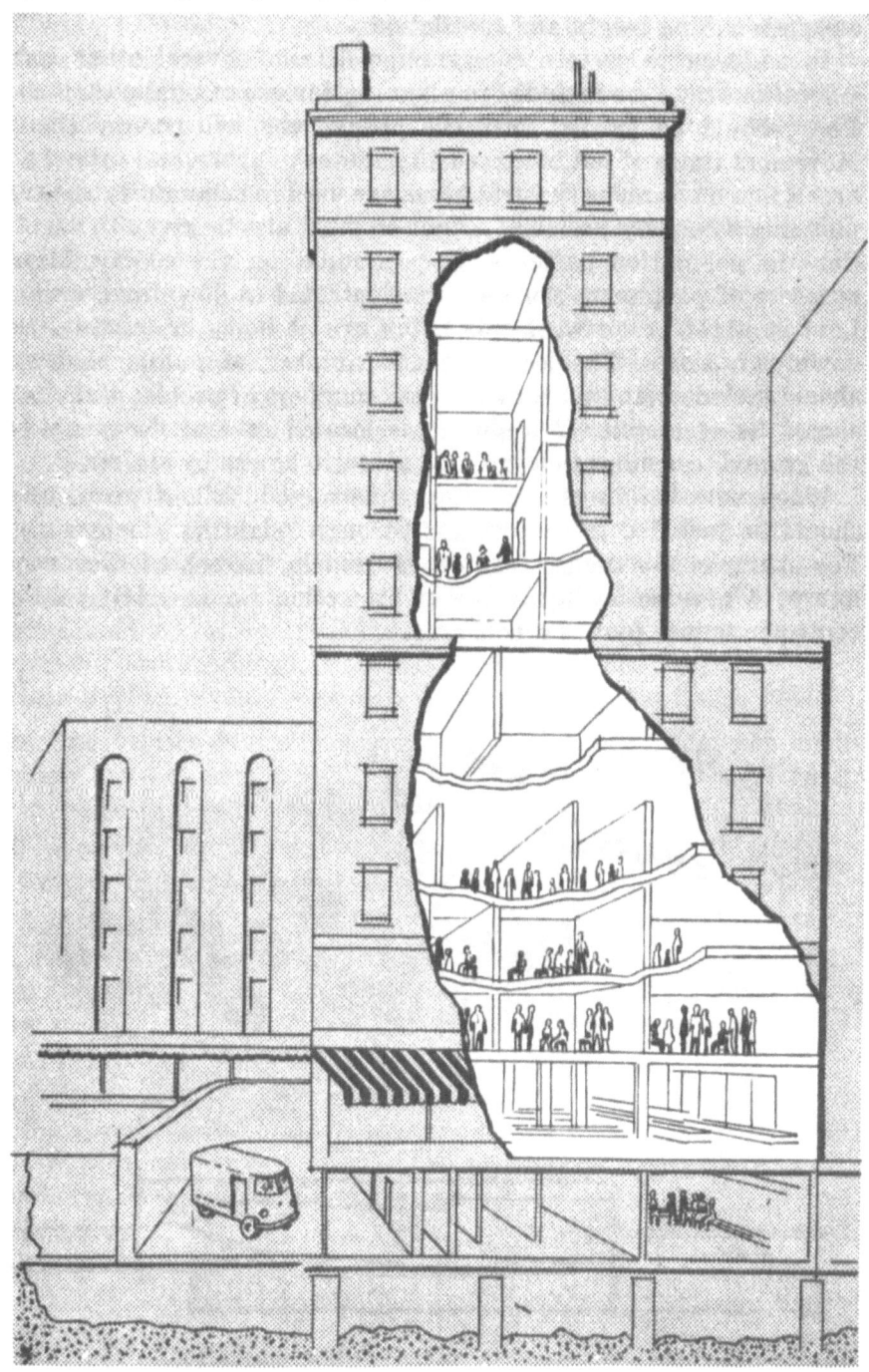

FIGURE 13.—Core shelter in a city office building.

A public shelter should provide the minimum essentials required to support life. There should be sufficient living area and adequate ventilation for the expected number of occupants. Ten square feet of floor space per person is normally planned, provided there is adequate ceiling height and ventilation.

In addition to certain construction details, several other considerations must be included in planning for use of public shelters. They should be located near the people who will occupy them. Movement times of not to exceed 30 minutes in urban and suburban areas, and 60 minutes in rural areas are used in community shelter planning whenever possible. Attention must also be given to variations in population patterns. For example, on a weekday, large numbers of people are normally concentrated in downtown areas. Late at night or on weekends many are at home or outside the downtown areas. The locations and number of public shelters should include planning for such peak numbers of people. A shelter should be accessible. If a shelter is located several floors above the ground, consideration must be given to access by stairway.

When new buildings are being constructed, fallout protection should be included in the designs through "slanting" techniques. For example, the design techniques used in the school shown in figure 14 provide adequate fallout protection for an additional 3 cents per square foot of school area.

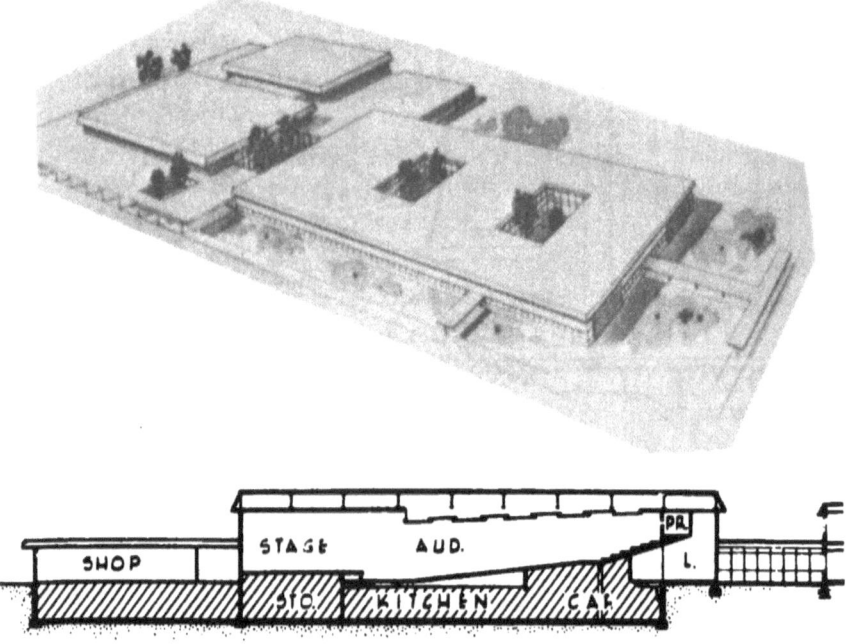

FIGURE 14.—Fallout shielding design in school buildings.

The school is essentially a two-story aboveground structure with a belowground basement which contains the cafeteria, kitchen, general food, and storage areas. Shelter is located in the basement area. Concrete was added to the floor of the shop and industrial arts wing to provide overhead protection to the general food and storage areas. In addition, by placing the cafeteria beneath the sloping, stepped concrete floor of the auditorium area, the architect was able to utilize normal structural components without modification to provide more shelter spaces.

The school has a capacity of 1,550, and in an emergency can shelter 1,761 persons. The shelter area has a protection factor of more than 100.

Many communities or neighborhoods need meeting places for various civic groups and local organizations. Others may require space for a community recreation hall or cafeteria or for public automobile parking. Teenagers often need a place for their after-school activities. A community center incorporating shelter can serve these and similar purposes.

The Office of Civil Defense has established a professional development service to encourage the incorporation of fallout shelter spaces in the design of new buildings and the remodeling of existing ones. Under this program, qualified instructors in the profession, and on the staffs of selected universities and colleges advise on how to design more protection into new buildings on request of State civil defense directors. Program activities include:

1. One or two-day seminars, courses, lectures, and on-the-job training sessions on fallout shelter analysis and design and criteria for architectural and engineering firms.

2. Review of building designs to evaluate potentials for fallout protection, and recommend slanting design techniques and other appropriate methods to integrate or improve shelter in the design.

3. Provision of technical guidance concerning the analysis, design, and construction of protective structures in order to maximize fallout radiation protection, utilizing slanting techniques where feasible.

4. Preparation of case studies, including preliminary plans, outline specifications, and preliminary cost estimates for alternate building designs for certain specified projects to incorporate protected areas suitable for use as shelters.

CHAPTER 4

FALLOUT SHELTER OCCUPANCY

During the time people must remain inside a shelter, they must be prepared to face and solve unfamiliar problems without outside assistance. As long as radiation levels in the area around the shelter are high, no outside help can be expected.

Local governments, with State and Office of Civil Defense assistance, are now training and assigning shelter managers for their public fallout shelters. In those shelters in which a manager has not been trained and assigned or in which the assigned manager is unable to reach the shelter, the people in the shelter must manage as best they can. In either case, the shelter area may be cramped, warm, stuffy, crowded, unfamiliar, lacking in privacy, and otherwise unpleasant. Past experience in wars and prolonged natural disasters indicate that people can and will live through such an experience. This experience is confirmed by experiments conducted by the Naval Radiological Defense Laboratory, American Institutes for Research, and the University of Georgia, where both selected groups and groups representative of the general population have successfully occupied fallout shelters for periods of up to 2 weeks. The balance of this chapter is devoted to some suggestions which the research would indicate will make such a period a little easier to live through.

The shelter manager, if available, and such staff as he may have will provide leadership for the occupants, but they will need the cooperation of all. The health, safety, and comfort of everyone depend on the situation and the degree to which shelter occupants cooperate with each other. Decisions will have to be made, several key functions will have to be staffed, and vital programs and activities will have to be commenced. These things cannot be done without each person doing his part.

One of the most effective ways to minimize anxiety is to keep busy. Everyone should be ready to perform any task within his capability, given him by the shelter manager or other leader, calmly and effectively. However, since a buildup of heat resulting from lack of space and body heat of the many occupants, and/or limited water supplies, may be a problem in many shelters, vigorous exercise or activity should be avoided. Other activities should be limited to those necessary for efficient operation of the shelter.

In some communities, space in shelters is being allocated in advance of emergency (see Ch. 6). In these communities, each person should learn the location of the shelter in which he is to seek protection if an attack warning is sounded. If an individual is far from his allocated shelter space when the warning signal is heard, he should seek protection in the nearest available shelter.

Know Shelter Location

At home, at work, at school, one should know the location of the nearest public shelter (fig. 15). Local civil defense authorities will advise you regarding those in your own community. Members of every family should learn the location of shelters in areas they frequent. When visiting a new or unfamiliar area, one would do well to make a point of noting nearby shelter markers.

FIGURE 15.—Become aware of public shelter locations.

If the warning signal is given, you should not pause to collect scattered belongings or unnecessary items—unless you are at home and plan to take shelter there. Hesitation will consume valuable time which may be needed in order to reach a shelter safely. In addition, it is probable that most space in a shelter will be required for the occupants and essential shelter stocks. There will be little room for personal possessions other than special medicines, drugs, or specific items needed by the individual or suggested by local civil defense authorities.

When an individual reaches shelter, some staff members may already be present. If so, they will probably assign people a place to sleep and to receive rations. Space will be at a premium, and existence in public shelter will be on an austere, survival basis. But the basic purpose of public fallout shelters—to save lives in event of nuclear attack—can be realized through cooperative effort. Consideration for others will be an important asset.

PSYCHOLOGICAL ASPECTS OF COMMUNITY SHELTER OCCUPANCY

During the period of shelter occupancy it is anticipated, based on extensive tests, that most people will be anxious but will still retain emotional self-control. There may, however, be people who will be more seriously disturbed. This condition may be brought on by the stress of the attack, unfamiliarity of shelter living, or by fear for the safety of missing relatives and friends. Abnormal or disturbed behavior will vary from individual to individual. Some may appear unusually excited. Some may be dazed, confused, or withdrawn. A few may exhibit only a slight nervous mannerism or tic. All in this group need help. Everyone must try to be tolerant of the situation. Some of these disturbed people will recover in a short time. A calm, optimistic, sympathetic, but unemotional acceptance of the situation will help considerably. These problems were met and surmounted by many occupants of shelters in London, Berlin, Tokyo, and elsewhere during World War II.

People under tension often need a chance to talk. They need simple tasks to take their minds off their experience and to give them a chance to get back their self-possession. If they receive no care, however, they may become a serious burden to the shelter community. Therefore, fellow shelter occupants should try to talk calmly and quietly to them, to establish sympathetic contact and, once contact has been made, to help them take part in some simple, helpful activity.

Generally, a layman should not try to administer sedatives or use physical force on emotionally disturbed people. They may even be harmed by shouts or slaps intended to "snap them out of it." Disturbed persons should not be blamed for their upset. A person's limitations are real; they should be recognized and accepted.

Wherever possible, special attention and encouragement should be given to elderly people and children. They should be given something useful to do if possible and shown that their help is appreciated.

Everyone must be prepared to make the best of life under conditions which are remote from the normal living pattern. There will probably be an annoying lack of privacy or a feeling of confinement. Everyone will be together day and night in the same limited area. Since each person must live, eat, and sleep here until it is safe to leave the shelter, he should be prepared to accept and cooperate with those around him, whoever they may be. Again, however, these conditions will be no worse than living conditions which thousands have undergone in peacetime catastrophes.

SUPPLIES IN PUBLIC SHELTERS

Food and Water Supplies

Most shelter occupants will be able to eat the food normally available in the building or available in shelter stocks being supplied by the Federal Government. Many marked shelter areas where food and water was not normally available are now specially provisioned with food and water or other standard supply items, and more are being stocked all the time. People who require a special diet, such as those who must eat salt-free or sugar-free foods, may need to bring their own supplies. Local civil defense officials can advise regarding local policies on bringing supplementary rations, bedding, or other supplies to shelter areas.

Cleaning and Special Personal Supplies

Basic medical and sanitation items are included in public shelter stocks. However, some people may wish to prepare a small emergency kit for personal hygiene, to be carried into shelter. Such items as special drugs or medicines, sanitary napkins, towels, and powder may be included. If there are infants or invalids in the family, certain items for their health or comfort could also be included. Local civil defense officials can advise concerning useful emergency items.

Clothing and Bedding

While most shelters will be quite warm, blankets to pad the floor, and extra clothing, may be useful additional items which the community may want people to bring into shelters.

CONTROL OF FOOD AND WATER IN SHELTERS

Food and water supplies may have to be carefully regulated by the trained shelter manager or other person in charge to ensure that they will last as long as needed. For the first few days after taking shelter, a system of food rationing may be required. This strict control over food and water will last only as long as necessary and may be relaxed when more information is available regarding probable length of shelter stay.

CARE OF THE SICK AND INJURED

The person in the shelter who is best qualified medically will supervise the care of the sick and injured.

It is quite possible that medical emergencies will be experienced during shelter occupancy. Some people will suffer from illnesses at the time they take shelter. Others may injure themselves. Childbirth will occur in some shelters, as it has in lifeboats, airplanes, and taxis. If sickness or injuries occur, the shelter staff should be notified immediately.

Effective quarantine will probably be impossible in most shelters because of space and facility limitations. However, it is desirable to keep the sick and injured in a separate area of the shelter, screened off, if possible, from other occupants. This procedure will facilitate their care and will minimize interference in other essential shelter activities.

Health and medical supplies in public shelters include self-help handbooks for treating sickness and injury. If necessary, they can be used to train shelter occupants who have had no previous instruction in these subjects.

SLEEPING IN COMMUNITY FALLOUT SHELTERS

Shelter stocks supplied by the Federal Government do not include sleeping equipment. In some cases, individuals may be asked to bring blankets with them to shelter. As bunks or cots probably will not be available, shelter occupants will have to sleep on the floor. A blanket, jacket, coat, or newspapers may serve as a pad or covering.

Depending on the configuration of each shelter, variations can be made in sleeping patterns. If, for example, there is a separate room connected to the main shelter area, people may sleep in shifts. While one group is sleeping, the remaining shelter occupants will be able to continue with other shelter activities.

SANITATION

Cleanliness and the proper disposal of wastes in shelter are vital to the prevention of disease; and here, even more than elsewhere, "an ounce of prevention is worth a pound of cure." During the period of shelter confinement, it will be important that occupants remain in as healthy a condition as possible. Medical supplies will be limited. If contagious illnesses break out in the confined space of the shelter, there may be no way to control them effectively.

It is the responsibility of every public shelter occupant to keep himself as clean as possible and to encourage those around him to be scrupulously clean during the entire period of shelter confinement. Limited supplies of disinfectants and water may prevent washing as often as desired, but full use should be made of cleaning opportunities. Special efforts should be made to keep the hands clean. Any disinfectants available should be appropriately used.

If the food supply is limited to the basic shelter "biscuits" and supplement, the cleaning problem after meals will be minimized. If more elaborate rations are available, there will be a greater problem in disposing of meal scraps. In any case, those responsible should do everything possible to keep areas where food is prepared and eaten free of crumbs and dirt. Latrine areas should also be regularly swept, mopped, and treated with a germicidal solution, if available. The entire shelter should receive a sanitary inspection at least once every day, by the assigned shelter manager or other person in charge, and the toilet area should be inspected at least twice daily.

USE OF TIME

Whether a family is preparing to go into a public shelter or to use fallout protection available in their home, there should be plans for activities which will help pass the time more quickly and help to prepare people for life in the postattack environment.

Shelter Amusements

The person arranging shelter amusements should choose games that will not require much activity or create too much noise when they are played, since it is important to avoid producing unnecessary heat; and shelter occupants may be ill or asleep at the time others want to play. Games likely to arouse arguments should be avoided. Those that can be played by one person or small groups will be especially useful.

Physical Exercise

In the postattack world, there will be a need for hard work and useful activity by everyone. Life in a shelter, however, with its limited room, can easily become an inactive existence resulting in stiff, sore muscles and physical weakness.

That is why all members of the group should engage in regular physical exercise while they are confined to the shelter. Everyone should do some simple exercises every day. However, rigorous and strenuous activities should be avoided, to prevent raising the shelter temperatures to uncomfortable levels and to prevent stimulating appetites for food and water.

Religious Activities

In any public shelter where no priest, minister, or rabbi is present, a layman should be in charge of religious activities. Keeping up religious observances during the period of shelter confinement can be a rich source of encouragement. Clergymen will be of great service in advising family members of appropriate and available spiritual helps.

PLANNING FOR LIFE OUTSIDE

During the period of public shelter occupancy, leaders may conduct group sessions to discuss problems of shelter living—including the shelter organization, individual and group responsibilities, the need for conserving supplies, and safety precautions. They may also devote attention to the situation that occupants may find outside the shelter. Groups may meet at "classes" to receive this information or, in some of the smaller public shelters, information may be presented to the entire population at one time.

The subjects discussed will vary with the situation but may include what is known about attack effects across the Nation, or locally, expected local fallout persistence, ways in which individuals can assist government recovery efforts when they emerge from shelter, and restorative actions that will be taken by the local, State, and Federal Governments. They may also include such subjects as home maintenance—wiring, plumbing, and structural repairs, etc.—preparation of food with limited facilities, or similarly useful material on personal living.

At a later time during the period of shelter confinement, small teams may leave the shelter for brief trips to get additional supplies, contact other shelters, or accomplish other tasks. Such trips should be planned carefully. Each trip should be evaluated in terms of goals, routes, numbers of people going, fallout radiation dangers, and times of expected return.

Similarly, family members in a home shelter should discuss the probable situation outside, dangers of the postattack environment, and family needs, before allowing anyone to emerge, however briefly. Of course, only when available radiological instruments indicate, or the radio has announced, that local radiation has reached relatively low levels should anyone plan to go out except for the most vital of reasons.

ADDITIONAL PREPARATORY TRAINING

This course provides a general orientation into civil defense, and points out things you can do for personal and family survival in emergency. Additional knowledge and skills that you can acquire will make you even better prepared. Useful skills that you might acquire, and which can be useful in daily peacetime living as well as during an attack emergency, include the capability to provide nonprofessional medical help to the sick and injured when no doctors or nurses are available, fire prevention and basic firefighting, simple rescue work, and the operation of communications equipment. Special training courses have been designed to enable individuals to acquire these and other emergency skills.

A Medical Self-Help Training Course has been developed by the Office of Civil Defense, and the Department of Health, Education, and Welfare, U.S. Public Health Service, in cooperation with the American Medical Association Council on National Security and Committee on Disaster Medical Care. This course includes information on caring for the sick and the injured, and on emergency childbirth. Information about the availability of this course may be obtained from local civil defense and public health organizations. Red Cross Chapters also offer a number of courses, such as first aid, home nursing, and mass feeding, which are of direct significance to civil defense work.

The local civil defense director can also furnish information about the training offered to shelter staff members. This training enables them, in time of emergency, to act as shelter managers, radiological monitors, or in other necessary capacities.

CHAPTER 5

FALLOUT PROTECTION AT HOME

In many parts of the country there is significant fallout protection available in existing homes. Since basement areas are furthest away from the source of fallout radiation and are located within a natural "shield," furnished by the masonry basement walls and the ground outside, they usually offer the best location in a house for fallout protection. A corner of a basement that is below ground level usually is better than the center of the basement.

Every house provides some degree of protection against fallout radiation. Some have inherent protection which even exceeds the minimum shelter criteria established by the Office of Civil Defense. Sample surveys, conducted for the Office of Civil Defense by the Bureau of the Census, indicate that 85 percent of those homes in the United States which have basements have corner areas that afford a protection factor of 20 or better. Shielding to upgrade the level of protection provided could be added in most of these homes.

Personal and other special considerations may make fallout protection at home more practical or desirable for certain individuals or families than protection in public shelters. For example, in small rural and suburban communities, families may live a considerable distance from the nearest public shelter. For these families, a home shelter will provide more accessible fallout protection. Fallout protection at home is often more accessible to housewives and young children during the day and to the whole family at night. Other families may prefer home fallout protection for personal reasons.

Evaluation of Fallout Protection in Homes

To assist those families that are planning to seek fallout protection at home, the Office of Civil Defense is initiating a survey system to analyze the fallout protection existing in 1-, 2-, and 3-family homes with basements. The survey will be made available on request to States in support of their community shelter planning efforts. This survey makes use of a simple questionnaire to be filled in by the homeowner or tenant. The questionnaire asks about location and building characteristics of the home. Completed questionnaires will be returned to the Federal Government for computer processing. A report will then be sent to the homeowner or tenant indicating the best protected portion of the basement and its approximate protection factor. Accompanying the report will be appropriate information for improving the fallout protection available in the home, if necessary. State and local governments will receive information for planning purposes on the *number* of homes in a community which offer good fallout protection, but *not* on which homes these are.

Improving Fallout Protection at Home

The ideas presented in the balance of this chapter will help you enhance the already existing fallout protection in your home. Prior to constructing any of the permanent-type shielding improvements, you should check to see that the design conforms to requirements of your local building code.

You can provide additional shielding for your basement by:

1. *Permanent Shelters.*—Making part of your basement into a shelter area or by building a permanent shelter which might also serve other purposes.
2. *Pre-planned Shelters.*—Locating shielding materials so that you can complete a shelter quickly in time of crisis.
3. *Improvised Shelters.*—Taking last-minute improvised actions if an emergency actually occurs.

The information contained on the following pages demonstrates some actions which you as a householder can take to provide fallout protection for yourself and your family.

In homes with basements, it is normally a simple and inexpensive matter to raise the protection factor to the recommended minimum of 40. Generally, in a home basement the least radiation protection is that provided by the roof and floors overhead against fallout on the roof. In protecting against the radiation coming in from fallout on the ground outside, the basement walls are of secondary importance to the shielding provided by the ground itself. The first step in improving the fallout protection in a home with a basement, therefore, is increasing the amount of overhead shielding.

A Word of Caution to the Home Handyman

Fallout Shelter Plans which follow are so simple that you may be tempted to construct them from the drawings in this booklet—and in many cases a thoroughly experienced "do-it-yourselfer" could do this. However, it requires very careful calculation of materials and fasteners to hold safely the heavy materials to be placed overhead. Therefore, it is strongly recommended that you build from the detailed plans and lists of materials which are available through the Home Fallout Protection Survey or the Office of Civil Defense. Before constructing any of the permanent shelters described here, you should check to see that the construction will conform to local building codes.

Figure 16 shows a permanent improvement which can be made in the fallout radiation shielding of your basement without affecting the use of the basement in any way.

All that is needed for this basement shielding improvement are some basic woodworking skills and approximately $165 for materials. The shelter can be incorporated while the basement is being built; or it can be added to an existing basement by modifying the ceiling in the corner which furnishes the best protection.

If the basement area is almost all below ground level, you can increase the fallout protection by installing bricks or solid concrete blocks between the wood joists in the best corner. The filler materials are supported by sheets of plywood fastened to the floor joists. A beam and screwjack column may be needed to keep the floor joists from bending too much. A carpenter can tell you if this is needed.

Plywood sheets (2' x 8' x ½" cut to fit) should be securely fastened to the joists, using 2-inch No. 8 screws 10 inches apart. Bricks or blocks are then packed as tightly as possible into the openings between the joists. Be sure to fill as much space as possible. To get the most protection out of this improvement, one-quarter of the basement ceiling over the best protected corner should be filled with bricks or solid concrete blocks.

A significant amount of protection can be achieved merely by inserting heavy material in the ceiling above the best corner. Light fixtures and installation of ceiling tiles or walls will raise the cost a bit, but you will be able to achieve a significant amount of protection without interfering with the functions of the basement.

Should the beam and screwjack column obstruct other planned uses for the basement, the alternate method of increasing overhead shielding shown in figure 17 may be the solution. Either of the methods should be applied to one-quarter of the basement ceiling over the best protected corner to achieve the most protection. More of the basement ceiling may be shielded if you wish. The alternate plan is so arranged that the shelter area can be enlarged at either end, depending upon the size of the basement.

The addition of two masonry walls (see "optional walls" in figure 16) to enclose the basement will provide an even greater amount of radiation protection.

Note: If too much of the basement wall is exposed (greater than 1 to 2 feet above grade), this plan will not provide sufficient protection. You should then use one of the other plans described in this manual.

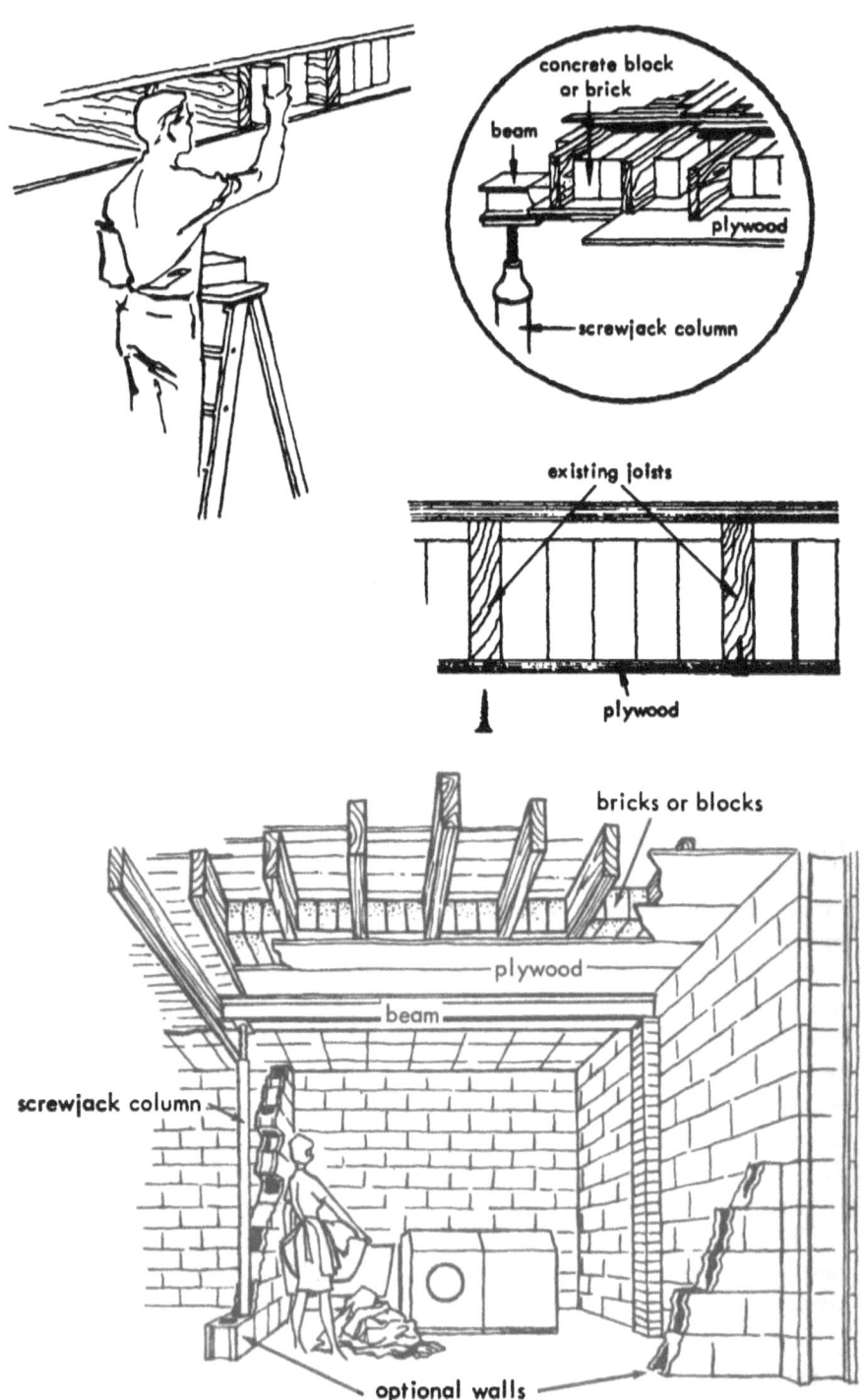

FIGURE 16.—Improving the overhead shielding in a home basement.

FIGURE 17.—An alternate method of increasing overhead shielding.

Wooden joists (2" x 12") which are notched at their ends for bearing are installed between existing floor joists (fig. 18). Plywood panels are then fastened to the 2- by 12-inch joists, and bricks or solid concrete blocks are packed into the open space between the joists (fig. 19). They are supported by the plywood panels. (Note: When existing joists are other than 10 inches deep, the notched joists should be 2 inches deeper; that is, 2" x 14"'s should be used with 2" x 12" existing joists.)

This type of construction does not require a beam and screwjack column to support the joists. The protected area can be used as a workshop, recreation room, pantry area, laundry room, or part of a family room. With ceiling tile covering the plywood panels, no one would recognize the area as a fallout shelter. Since the objective is to provide as much overhead mass as possible, the heaviest weight of solid brick or block (placed on end if possible) should be used.

Figure 20 shows addition of joists and bricks for basement corner shielding.

If your basement is not completely below grade, here are some additional ideas which can be used to increase the shielding of exposed basement walls:

A brick or stone planter box along one or more sides of the house will improve the protection substantially, and will provide

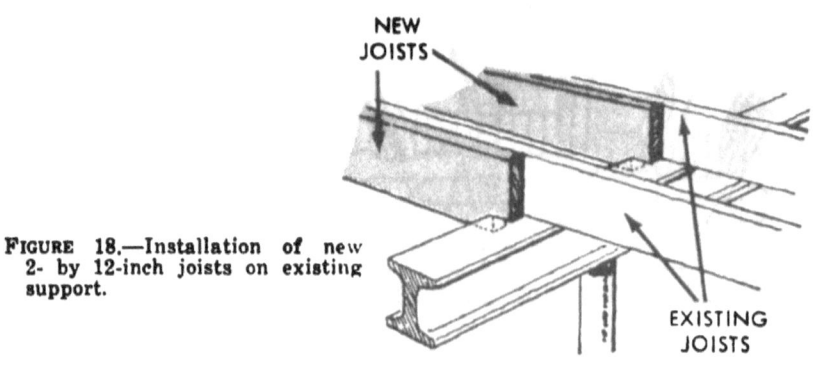

FIGURE 18.—Installation of new 2- by 12-inch joists on existing support.

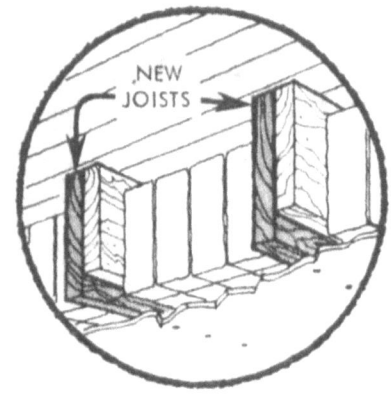

FIGURE 19.—Filling void spaces between 10- and 12-inch joists.

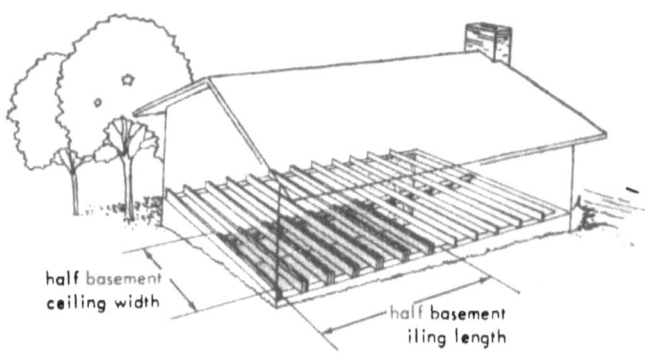

FIGURE 20.—Addition of joists and bricks for basement corner shielding.

an attractive setting for small shrubs and perennials as well. If the partially exposed wall is at the rear or side of the house, an elevated garden could be built with masonry retaining walls. (See fig. 21.)

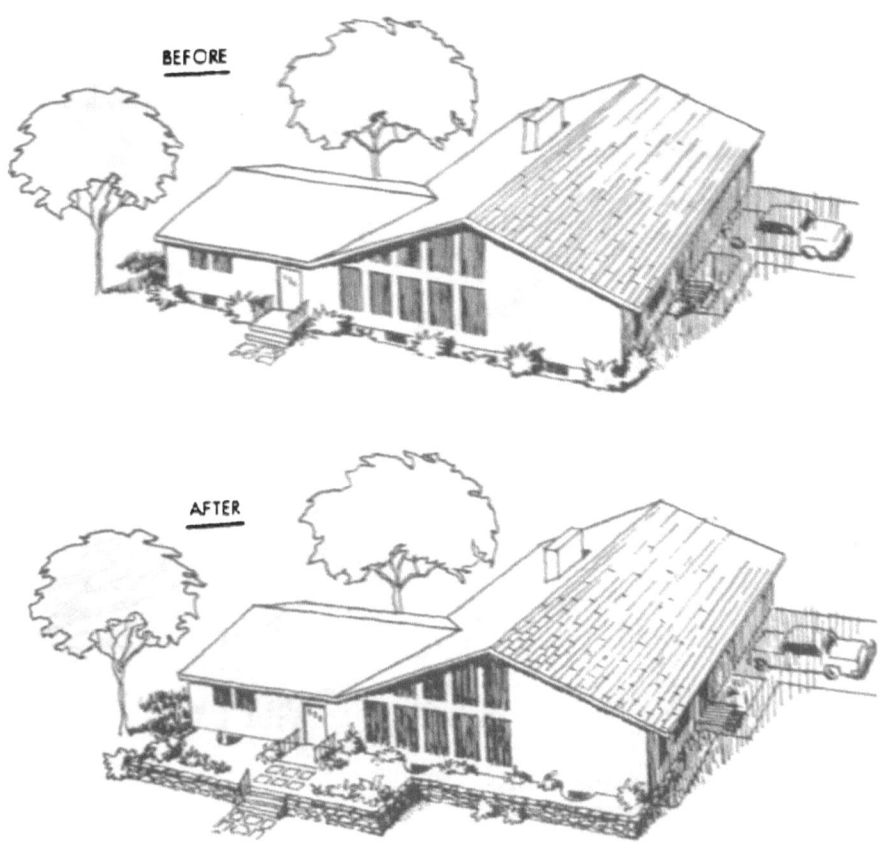

FIGURE 21.—An elevated planting area used to increase the shielding provided by a partially exposed basement wall.

If the partially exposed walls have windows, these can still be used by providing window wells within the planter box or elevated garden area. Your basement's PF will also be increased by providing additional shielding to the exposed section. This can be done by piling patio block, sand, earth, cordwood, or similar materials against the exposed wall as shown in figure 22.

Enclosing your patio area with a solid masonry screen wall will give you privacy for lounging and cookouts and will provide a barrier shield to increase the protection factor in the basement area. (See fig. 23.)

A snack bar built of brick or solid block can be converted into a fallout shelter in a short period of time by lowering a strong hinged false ceiling to rest on the snack bar. The false ceiling section can then be loaded with brick or solid block. The brick or blocks can be conveniently stored by incorporating them into recreation room furniture, such as benches, room dividers, etc. Figure 24 illustrates this design.

If the partially exposed walls have windows, these can still be used by providing window wells within the planter box or elevated garden area.

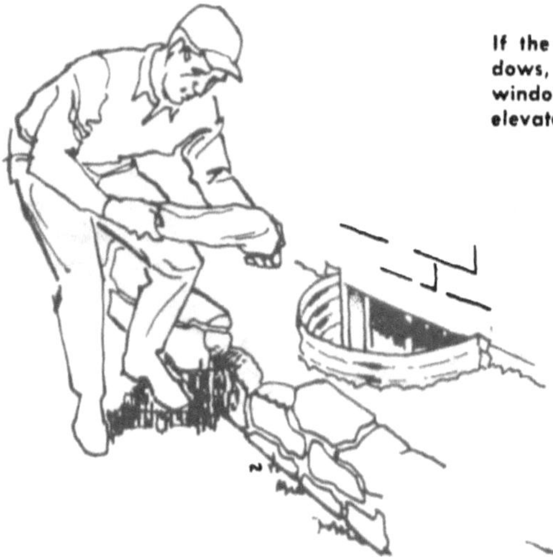

The fallout protection of your basement will also be increased by providing additional shielding to the exposed section. This can be done by piling patio block, sand, earth, cordwood or similar materials against the exposed wall.

FIGURE 22.—Methods of providing shielding at basement windows and along exposed basement walls.

FIGURE 23.—A patio screen wall provides additional shielding along an exposed basement wall.

FIGURE 24.—A recreation room snack bar that provides fallout protection.

A concrete block shelter, as shown in figure 25, will provide excellent low-cost protection from the effects of radioactive fallout. Even if your home has very little existing shelter space, this shelter will provide, in most cases, a protection factor of 100 or more. The shelter is intended to be installed in the corner of your basement having the highest protection. Its principal advantages are simple design, speed of construction, and ready availability of low-cost materials. It can be designed as a sit-down shelter; or, if the ceiling height is increased to 6 feet or more, it could be a more comfortable shelter and serve a dual-purpose as a storage room or similar facility. Natural ventilation is provided by the entrance and the air vents in the shelter wall. This type of shelter will cost an estimated $135 to $150, depending on its height.

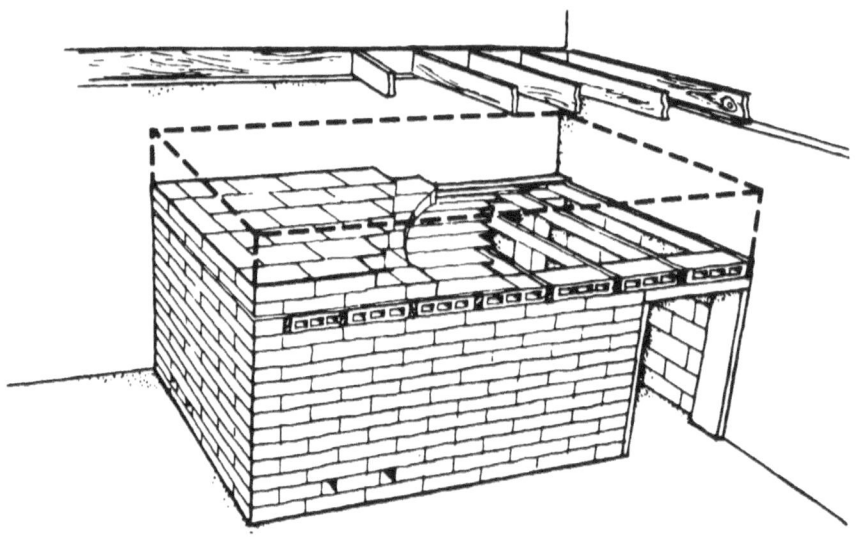

FIGURE 25.—A basement concrete block shelter.

If your basement is below or nearly below ground level on three sides and exposed on one side (as with "walk-in" basements), this design—and other permanent shelter designs—must be modified to achieve the desired effectiveness as shown in figure 26. The following changes should be made:

1. Increase the thickness of the shelter wall facing the basement wall which has no ground cover by 4 inches of brick, concrete block, or similar materials.
2. Place the entrance to the protected area on a side or end which does *not* face the exposed basement wall.

Improvising Fallout Protection in a Basement

If a public shelter is not available and you have not provided your own fallout shelter, what would you do if you suddenly heard that the United States had been attacked with nuclear weapons?

You can still protect yourself and your family if you know what to do and if you act quickly. Pick out the corner of your basement with the highest ground level outside. That is the safest place in the basement. **Now Make it Safer.**

If you have a sturdy table or workbench, place it in the corner. Quickly fill drawers or boxes with the heaviest material readily

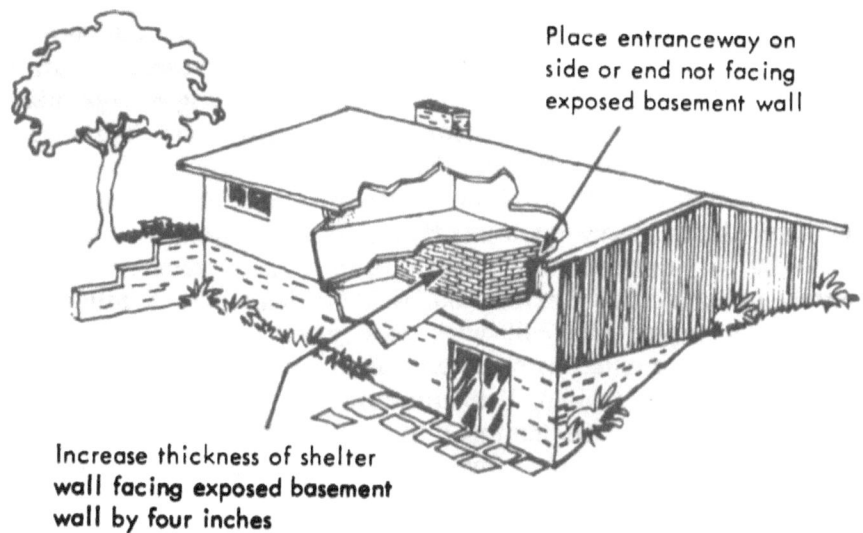

Place entranceway on side or end not facing exposed basement wall

Increase thickness of shelter wall facing exposed basement wall by four inches

FIGURE 26.—Recommended additional improvements to fallout protection in walk-in basements.

available—sand or dirt, bricks—or if you have nothing heavier, newspapers or books. Stack these materials on the top and the sides of the table or workbench.

In belowground basements, it is most important to have shielding overhead. Place most of the material there.

Be careful not to overload the table or bench to a point where it will collapse. Figure 27 shows a man improvising fallout protection in this manner.

FIGURE 27.—Improvising fallout protection in a basement, using a workbench.

63

If a workbench is not available, you can improvise a somewhat larger shelter area by using furniture, doors, dressers, or other materials (fig. 28). Remove doors from their hinges and place them over supports in the corner of your basement having the best protection. The supports for this improvised table can be chests of drawers, or anything that can take a heavy load. Two or three doors placed one atop the other should provide sufficient strength to support heavy loads. Place bricks, concrete blocks, earth- or sand-filled drawers, books and magazines, a collapsible children's wading pool (fill with water when in place), etc., over the doors to provide an overhead shield; and along the sides to provide a vertical shield. Use anything with weight that can be moved. The heavier the material, the better the protection. **Again, however, be careful not to overload the doors to the point where they will collapse.**

FIGURE 28.—An improvised basement shelter.

To help you avoid overloading the top supports of your improvised shelter, the brief list at the top of the next page gives the approximate weights per square foot of typical shielding materials of 4-inch thickness:

MATERIAL	APPROX. WT. (lb. per sq. ft.)
Earth or sand	35
Wood	10
Water	21
Cinder blocks	22
Bricks	32
Solid concrete blocks	48
Books	15

Homes Without Basements

Few homes without basements provide adequate fallout protection. Therefore, if your home does not have a basement, you should plan other fallout protection if possible. There may be public fallout shelter which you can use. If not, you may be able to make use of fallout protection in a building near your home. Friends and neighbors, for example, may arrange to gather together for fallout protection in the home of one of the families that has a basement.

If these solutions are not feasible, the best means of providing adequate fallout protection, in the absence of a basement, is the construction of a low-cost fallout shelter in the backyard. Figure 29 shows two such low-cost shelters. The plywood box shelter will cost about $100 for materials, while the steel culvert materials will cost about $150. Both of these shelters may be enlarged to provide for more people or greater comfort at a corresponding increase in cost.

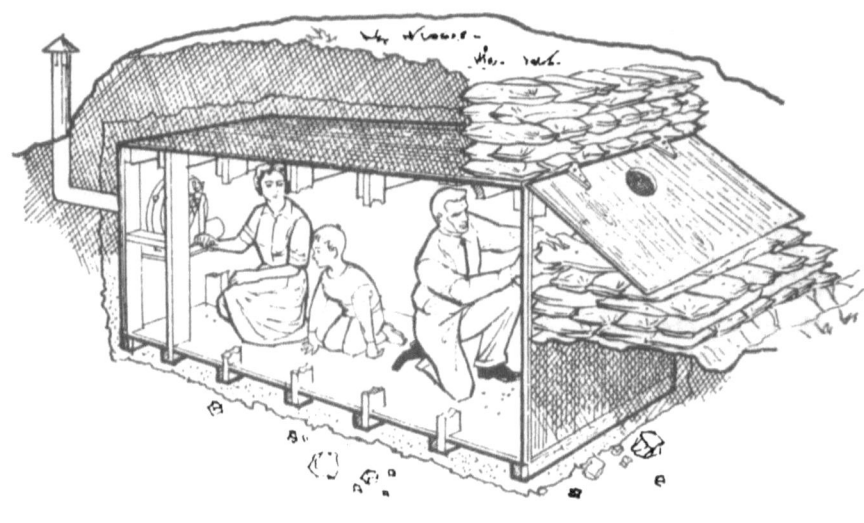

Figure 29.—Two low-cost backyard fallout shelters.

Plans for these and other shelters are available from your local civil defense director.

Improvising Fallout Protection Without Basements

If you do not have a public shelter available to you, your home does not have a basement, and you have not provided yourself with a fallout shelter, there are still last-minute actions which you can take to gain some fallout protection. While uncomfortable, and in some cases offering less protection than is desirable, such improvised shelter could save your life.

There are basically two methods of improvising fallout protection if your home doesn't have a basement. One method is for use inside the home—the other, outside. To improvise fallout protection inside your home, first select the area having the greatest inherent fallout protection. This will normally be in a hallway or room near the center of the ground floor. In this area, place the largest and strongest table or similar piece of furniture that will fit. By using other furniture and doors already available, it may be possible to improvise such a table. Then put as much heavy furniture, books, magazines, boxes or drawers of sand or earth, and other heavy materials as you safely can on top of and around the table. Unlike the basement workbench improvised shelter, you will need about as much shielding material around your ground floor improvised shelter as on top of it.

If you have a space problem on one or more sides of your improvised shelter, as might be the case in a central hall, the shielding for that side may be placed in an adjoining room against the wall near the shelter area. This type of improvised shelter is shown in Figure 30.

For use outside a basementless house, a simple and effective lean-to shelter can be built by constructing the components and storing them where they can be quickly assembled against the side of the house in emergency. Components consist of a frame and filler materials such as brick, solid concrete blocks, or patio blocks. The fillers can be put to use as patio paving or garden walks set loosely in sand—to be taken up and used for completing this shelter in an emergency, as shown in figure 31. Detailed plans for such a shelter can be obtained as outlined on page 54.

Another way to improvise fallout protection outside is to dig a trench. To limit the time required to complete this work, the trench should be kept as small as possible, commensurate with the number of people who will occupy it. Be sure to keep the trench narrow enough that the doors or other material which will be used to support the overhead cover will have ample bearing surface on each side. As the trench is dug, pile the loose soil, which has been excavated, nearby as it will be used to provide overhead protection. It is desirable to dig a short additional section of trench at a right angle to one end of the main trench to serve as an entrance and to provide ventilation, while keeping the protection against radiation up to acceptable levels. If the trench is being dug in particularly loose or sandy soil, it may be necessary to support the walls of the trench with doors, fencing, or similar available materials.

When the digging and any necessary shoring of the walls of the trench is completed, doors, bed rails, table tops, or similar supports should be placed over the trench. Then the loose soil from the trench should be piled on top of these supports. Care should be taken to see that this overhead cover of soil is at least a foot

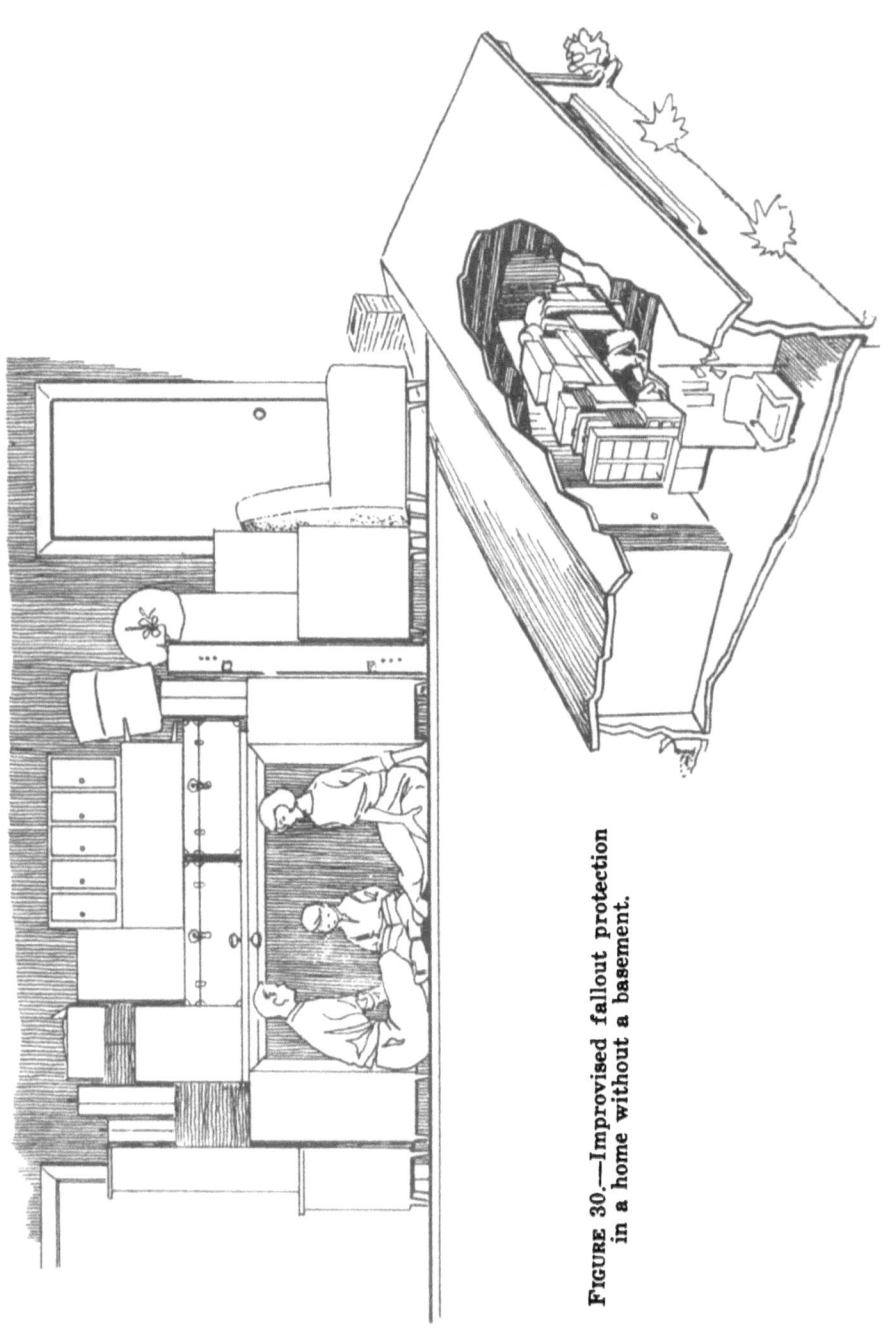

FIGURE 30.—Improvised fallout protection in a home without a basement.

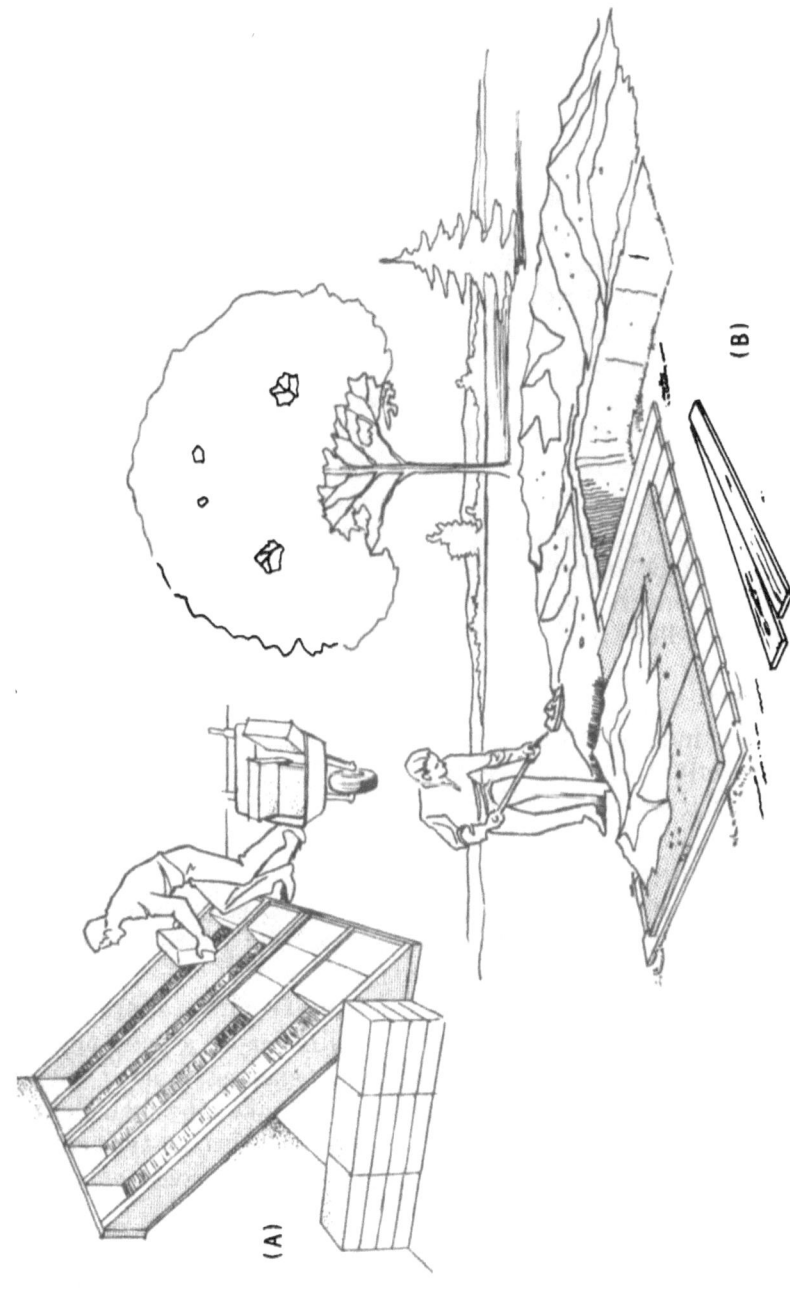

FIGURE 31.—Improvising fallout protection: (a) Lean-to shelter that can be constructed in a basement or outside the house; (b) "L" shaped trench.

thick at all points, but not so heavy as to cause the supporting material to collapse. If time permits, this overhead cover should be graded into a smooth mound to cause rain or melting snow to drain away from the trench.

Lighting

Plans for home fallout protection should include provisions for continuous low-level lighting in the shelter area, since, in total darkness, many people might find shelter life unbearable. Brighter light will be needed occasionally for reading or for emergencies. Candles, kerosene, or gasoline-burning lamps should be used with care in a home shelter, as in very crowded or poorly ventilated areas they may constitute a carbon monoxide or fire hazard.

After a nuclear attack, many community electric power services may continue to function. Light and power outlets from the house electrical circuits, if not already present, should be installed in every home shelter. If electric power from the house circuits can be used, light can be furnished in a normal manner. Nevertheless, fresh batteries should be kept in the shelter to provide light if normal electrical power fails. The effectiveness of shelter light sources can be increased by painting the shelter ceiling white. In addition, metal or metallic foil reflectors should be installed behind each light bulb for greater lighting efficiency.

Ventilation

The air in most basement shelter areas probably would circulate by convection currents. No ventilation system power is required for such natural circulation. It is unlikely that fallout will get into these basement shelter areas in any considerable amount because of the structure above and around the shelter.

A blower or forced-air system requiring an air-circulating pump is needed in home underground shelters, and might be desirable in a basement shelter for increased comfort.

In home underground shelters, an intake pipe (approx. 3-in.) may be installed to lead in fresh air by means of a hand-operated blower that is cranked periodically. An exhaust pipe or opening would be needed to vent stale air. The air-intake pipe should extend about 2 feet above the ground and have a mushroom-type cap and a screen. This gives the protection required to keep out fallout particles.

Heating

In most areas of the United States, a space-heating unit for the shelter is not needed. The body heat of the inhabitants will usually keep the shelter warm. In areas where severe cold (0°F and below) is common in winter, an electric space heater may be provided to increase comfort.

Reduction of Combustible Material

Reducing the amount of combustible material in the shelter construction and contents will increase the safety of the occupants. Practical measures include the use of noncombustible furnishings, noncombustible containers for storage of food and supplies, use of wool blankets in preference to cotton or certain synthetic fabrics, use of canvas cots in place of mattresses, and storage of combustible waste in metal containers with tight lids until disposal outside shelter is feasible.

The occupants of family shelters must be prepared to extinguish small fires quickly and, if feasible, to ventilate the shelter. Because they are very hazardous in confined spaces, carbon tetrachloride extinguishers should *not* be used in shelters. Plans should be made for the possible use of other shelter or refuge in the event that fires or noxious and lethal fumes make it necessary to leave.

BASIC SUPPLIES AND EQUIPMENT

During the design and development of a fallout shelter in a home, provisions should be made for storage of such necessary equipment as food, water, fire-protection equipment, and battery radios.

Water

A dependable water supply is essential to a family shelter. A supply of at least a quart, but preferably about a gallon, a day per occupant should be sufficient for drinking and washing needs. Some water is also needed for general sanitary purposes. The basic supply of water should be inside the shelter.

Although large bottles do not take up as much floor or shelf space as smaller ones required to store the same volume, they are usually difficult to lift, and the risk of spilling precious water or breaking the bottle is high.

Covered 1- or 2-gallon plastic containers are recommended for the home shelter water supply. Plastic containers may affect the taste of the water in time, but the change is harmless, and such containers have a great advantage in that they seldom break when they are dropped. As each container is emptied it can be used to store waste water and fluids.

Additional water for shelter use could be obtained from the household water tanks. If a gravity storage tank or hot water tank is not far from the shelter entry, a pipe and faucet can be installed from the tank to the shelter. If the water system is shut off, an upstairs faucet must be opened to relieve the vacuum. Water that has been carefully stored for long periods of time will be as safe to drink as fresh water but may not taste "fresh." Some may want to test their stored water for smell and taste every 3 months, but it is not necessary for health. Odorous as it might become, it will still be usable in an emergency.

Food

Assuming that sufficient water is available, most people could survive in a fallout shelter for a period of 2 weeks without any food. However, families able to maintain anything like normal dietary practices would have significantly less difficulty in maintaining good health and good spirits. This is particularly true if care is taken to make ample provision for the special needs of infants, invalids, and others on special diets.

It is desirable that the food stock supply each family member with a minimum of 2,000 calories per day (about two-thirds of average normal intake) for a period of 2 weeks. As a matter of fact, the family fallout shelter food supply need be limited only by space and financial ability to buy food in excess of immediate needs. Naturally, the entire stock need not be purchased at once, but can be accumulated a few items at a time over a period of several months.

Family food preference is an important consideration in choosing foods to be stocked in the home shelter. Properly canned or packaged foods retain a fresh taste for months, sometimes years, but it is recommended that shelter food supplies be used frequently for regular family meals and replaced, so that shelter stocks are always relatively fresh.

Food should be stored in the shelter according to its estimated shelf life. In general, juices have the shortest shelf life, while products canned in oil have the longest.

Some foods that are easy to store and have high food value should be stored to supplement the more normal favorites. Powdered milk should be stocked, along with small cans of evaporated milk.

Small cans and packages of food are generally to be preferred over larger sizes, so that when they are opened all the contents will be eaten at a single meal. The water supply should be supplemented with bottled and canned beverages, including fruit and vegetable juices. Precooked foods and those that require little or no heating should be chosen in preference to other foods. Cooking or warming of food in shelter should be restricted to avoid unnecessary buildup of heat. Can and bottle openers should not be forgotten! A knife, a screwdriver, or any sharp object might serve as a makeshift can or bottle opener, but they certainly are not easy to use.

It may be necessary to leave the shelter quickly. After the attack, a family may suddenly have to move to another location. Therefore, if the supplies of food and water have been kept in boxes, trays, or other containers, they can be carried to a waiting car or truck without delay.

Suggestions for the shelter food supply are listed below:

SUGGESTIONS FOR SHELTER BASIC FOOD SUPPLY

Food	Amount required daily for 1 person	Quantity required for 2 weeks	2-week supply of standard-size containers	Maximum shelf life (months)
Staples:				
Crackers, cookies, pretzels	4 oz.	56 oz.	2 cans or jars	36
Candy:				
(chocolate bars, hard candies)	1 oz.	16 oz.	1-lb. jar or box	18
Sugar	2 tsp.	4 oz.	¼ lb. (lb. per 4 persons).	36
Salt	2 tsp.	4 oz.	¼ lb. (lb. per 4 persons).	Indefinite.
Beverages:				
Instant coffee or tea	2 cups.	2 oz.	2 jars	Indefinite.
or				
Chocolate	2 cups.	4 oz.	2 (1-lb.) pkgs.	Indefinite.
or				
Soft drinks	1½ bottles.		24 bottles.	Indefinite.
Milk:				
Nonfat, dry	⅓ cup.	20 oz.	2 pkgs.	
Evaporated	1 oz. (2 tbsp.).	14 oz.	4 cans	48
Juices:				
Orange, tomato, grapefruit, pineapple.	½ cup.	64 oz.	6 bottles	36
Fruits:				
Peaches, pears, prunes, apricots.	1 cup.	112 oz.	4 jars or 2 (1-lb.) pkgs.	36–40
Vegetables:				
Peas, corn, lima beans	½ cup.	112 oz.	8 cans	60
Soups:				
Vegetable, pea, noodle, beef, clam chowder, mushroom, other than tomato.	1 cup.	112 oz.	8 cans	36
Meats and substitutes:	1 cup.	208 oz.	8 (1-lb. and ½-lb.) cans.	36–48
Canned beef stew, salmon, tuna, spaghetti and meatballs, baked beans and frankfurters (without tomato sauce), chicken and noodles.				
Other foods:				
Cheese, peanut butter		7 oz.	4 jars	
Jam, jelly, marmalade		7 oz.	2 jars	24–30
Cereals			14 pkgs. (individual serving size).	

The amounts per person listed in the table are based upon menus that provide 2,000 calories per day. It is important to remember that some items, such as fruit juices, are corrosive. Foods preserved in glass containers will have a long shelf life. Crown-capped bottles of fruit juices, and fruits and vegetables in glass jars, preferably with glass lids, are long shelf-life items that are easily obtainable. All containers should be stored in an upright position. Precautions against breakage should be taken.

In addition to a food stock and can openers, equipment for cooking and serving is desirable. Some cooking pans, disposable tableware—including paper plates, cups, and napkins—a measuring cup, and a small electric food-heating unit should be stored in the shelter area. A small camp stove can be provided for use if heat is not a problem and ventilation is adequate after the period of continuous shelter occupancy has ended. Cooking should be done outside the shelter area to avoid potential problems of heat, carbon monoxide, and carbon dioxide in the relatively confined shelter space. To avoid a possible fire hazard, large amounts of fuel should not be stored in the shelter.

First Aid and Medical Supplies

A first aid kit and instruction booklet belongs in the shelter area. Supplies should be checked and renewed as necessary every few months. If some members of the family are allergic to certain medicines, their allergies should be considered when stocking the first aid kit. Since most drugs are potentially dangerous, they should be stored out of the reach of children.

Medical supplies must be tailored to individual needs of the family. However, the following basic list will be helpful in preparing to meet those needs:

Antiseptic solution
Aspirin tablets (5-grain)
Baking soda
Cough mixture
Diarrhea medication
Ear drops
Table salt
Toothache remedy
First aid handbook
Specific medications recommended by your physician
Adhesive tape, roll (2" wide)
Applicators, sterile, cotton-tipped
Bandage, sterile roll (2" wide)
Bandage, sterile roll (4" wide)
Bandages, triangular (37"x37"x52")
Bandages (can of plastic strips, assorted sizes)
Cotton, sterile, absorbent
Laxative
Motion sickness tablets (for nausea)
Nose drops (water soluble)
Petroleum jelly
Rubbing alcohol
Smelling salts
Dressings, sterile (4" x 4")
Safety pins (assorted sizes)
Sanitary napkins
Soap
Scissors
Splints, wooden (18" long)
Thermometer (clinical oral or rectal type)
Tweezers
Water purification materials
Handbook on family health and first aid, such as:
"Family Guide: Emergency Health Care" (DHEW)
Red Cross textbook, "Home Nursing;" or Instructor's Guide, "Care of Sick and Injured."

Sanitary Supplies

The shelter should contain sanitary supplies such as toilet tissue, paper napkins, paper towels, plastic and paper bags, clean rags, newspapers, sanitary napkins, waterproof gloves, disinfectants, insecticides, and one or two scrubbing brushes.

Soap and detergents are very useful shelter supplies. A small basin and a sponge or two will prove their worth, and so-called dry washcloths (paper impregnated with soap) are very useful shelter items.

Hairbrushes could be helpful in removing fallout from the person. Shaving supplies, combs, cosmetics, and other grooming aids are certainly not essential shelter supplies, but may contribute towards maintaining morale.

Cleanliness is important, particularly in time of disaster and in relatively crowded living conditions such as will be common in shelter areas. Cleanliness is important not only to comfort and morale but also to reduce the probability of disease.

Plans should be made to handle the disposal of human wastes. A simple means is a metal pail with a tight cover. A better expedient, especially where elderly persons are involved, is a commode made by cutting the seat out of a chair and placing a pail under it. In either case, a supply of plastic bags, obtainable at department stores, is desirable. Each bag, placed in the pail with the top of the bag overlapping the pail rim, serves as a pail liner and is easily disposable. A small amount of disinfectant (creosol or household bleach) will help control odors and insect breeding.

A large can with a cover, such as a garbage can, should be available to store the plastic bags after use. After 2 days the container can be placed outside the shelter. At a later time, the waste should be buried under 1 or 2 feet of earth.

Garbage and Rubbish Disposal Equipment

A home shelter should contain two or more garbage cans, with lids wired or tied to the cans. A tight-fitting lid is important to keep out flies and other insects and to prevent undesirable odors from escaping from the can.

If liquids are drained off, garbage may be stored for a long period without developing an unpleasant odor. After liquids are drained off, the garbage should be put into a plastic bag or wrapped in several thicknesses of newspaper before placing it in a container. The wrapping will absorb the remaining moisture. (See fig. 32.)

Special Supplies

As in the case of public shelters, if there are diabetics, chronic

FOR PROPER SEWAGE AND GARBAGE DISPOSAL YOU WILL NEED...

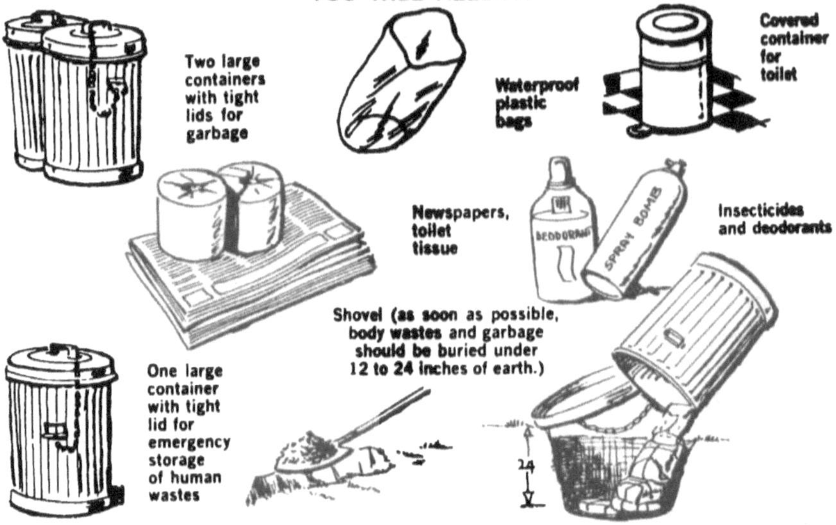

Two large containers with tight lids for garbage

Waterproof plastic bags

Covered container for toilet

Newspapers, toilet tissue

Insecticides and deodorants

One large container with tight lid for emergency storage of human wastes

Shovel (as soon as possible, body wastes and garbage should be buried under 12 to 24 inches of earth.)

FIGURE 32.—Sewage and garbage disposal.

invalids, aged or infirm persons in the family, any special medicines or equipment they will need should be placed in the shelter area. The person who is stocking the shelter should keep in mind all special diet problems. Canned or powdered milk, baby bottles, disposable diapers, and other special supplies should be included for infants.

After the shelter area has been equipped for emergencies, the family may want to place in it other appliances or equipment that would enable them to get more everyday enjoyment out of the room. There is no reason for not installing a television set, a record player, or a telephone in the shelter area, if these items do not take up space that will be required when the shelter is needed for emergency purposes. Books and family photograph albums stored on the shelves of a shelter area will provide hours of relaxation during both ordinary and emergency situations.

It is a good idea to keep the family strongbox in the shelter. The box should contain copies of wills, deeds, and other personal property, banking and other fiscal records, marriage and birth certificates, insurance papers, savings bonds, other securities, and similar important papers. In normal circumstances, the shelter area is a safe, out-of-the-way location for these records; in a disaster or postdisaster period, the shelter area probably is the best home location for important records. Consideration should also be given to storing additional copies of such essential records in a bank safety deposit box.

Battery-Operated Radio

A battery-operated radio is an important item of shelter equipment. The information received by radio in an emergency may spell the difference between life and death. A transistorized portable radio is preferred because its low power drain results in longer battery life.

The strength of radio signals is sometimes reduced by the shielding necessary to keep out radiation. As soon as the shelter area is complete, a radio reception check must be made. It may be necessary to install an outside antenna to receive emergency broadcasts. It would be helpful to keep an extra indoor antenna in the shelter in case an antenna must be improvised.

Radiation Meters

Because gamma rays cannot be detected by any of the five senses, each home shelter should have simple instruments to detect and measure them. (See p. 29 for information on the citizens radiation-monitoring instrument kit.) Possession of these instruments does not automatically provide simple solutions to problems of radiation exposure, since the relationships between dose rate, total dose, time, and radioactive decay must be learned. Instructions are normally included with instruments on how to interpret the readings. Familiarity with their use obviously would be of the greatest value in planning intelligent courses of action to be taken in a fallout situation.

Clothing and Bedding

A change of clothing for each member of the family might be kept in the shelter area. Changing clothes during a shelter stay of 10 days to 2 weeks would be a material aid to comfort and morale.

During winter months in cold climates, enough blankets and heavy outer clothing should be kept in the shelter to keep each occupant warm without artificial heat.

If there is dampness in the shelter area, the clothing and bedding stored there must be protected from mildew.

Rescue Tools

Before, during, or after a stay in a shelter, persons trapped in wreckage might have to be freed. Tools that can be used for rescue work therefore belong in the shelter. Priority should be given to a shovel, a coil of rope at least 25 feet long, and a crowbar. A broom, a bucket, a large pocket knife, an axe, a wrench, a screwdriver, a hammer, and a pair of pliers should also be stored in or near the shelter.

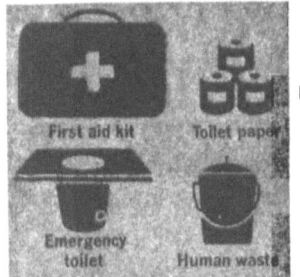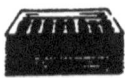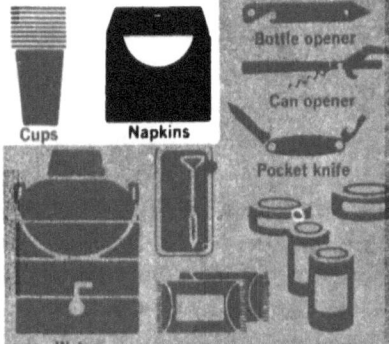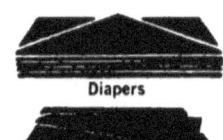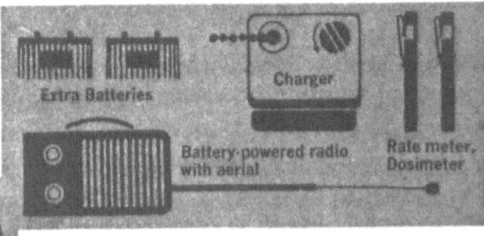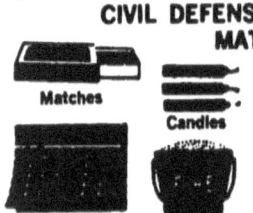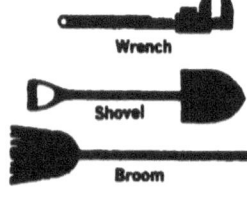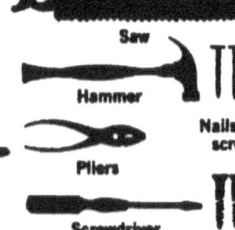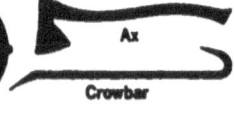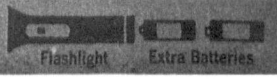

FIGURE 33.—Shelter supplies.

Summary on Supplies

Not every item on the chart in figure 33 is vital to survival. (The most essential ones are framed with gray tone.) Even though it might be possible to leave the shelter briefly a day or two after an attack everyone should prepare to be completely self-sustaining for at least 2 weeks.

The one essential item is water.

Some items such as tools should be kept handy but need not be inside the shelter itself.

SHELTER MAINTENANCE

The family fallout shelter will be ready for use in an emergency if it receives regular housekeeping attention. The shelter should always be clean and uncluttered and should not be used as a storage catchall. You and members of your family should hold inspections regularly to see that essential items are in clean, usable condition, and in their proper places. You should also hold practice shelter-use drills periodically. Each family member should be assigned responsibility for inspection and maintenance of essential items, and for emergency duties. The Appendix to this manual provides a checklist to help you in your planning.

PERSONAL EMERGENCY ACTIONS

While it is very unlikely that a nuclear war would begin without warning, it is possible that the first you would know of nuclear attack could be the flash of an explosion. If so, quick action during the next few seconds is essential. People who are inside should move under or behind the nearest desk, table, sofa, or other piece of sturdy furniture. This action will provide some degree of shielding from the thermal (heat) rays. The safest position to assume is lying down, curled up on one side with hands over the back of the neck, knees tucked against the chest. Stay away from windows and doors in order to avoid the thermal rays and flying glass.

People caught outside should run into a building and assume the same curled-up position, preferably in and facing a corner.

If it is not possible to get into a building quickly, the lowest, most protected spot, such as a ditch, gutter, or depression in a lawn should be sought. Again, the curled-up position is the safest. The face should be turned away from the flash.

People driving an automobile should stop immediately and get into a ditch or depression until 5 minutes after the explosion. Those people who are far enough away from the explosion may feel no effect at all. But they should stay put for 5 minutes to be sure.

The time available to find protection from fallout depends upon a number of variables. The key considerations are to take shelter in a building or other structure as soon as possible and to keep radiation exposure to a minimum.

Upon warning of attack—and if there is time before seeking shelter—householders should quickly guard against the hazards of fires that could be set by the heat of a nuclear explosion. Shut off household appliances. If there are venetian blinds at the windows, lower and shut them to bar flying glass and to screen out some of the nuclear heat. Fill buckets, sinks, bathtubs, or other available containers with water.

You should keep these six general guidelines in mind in seeking last-minute fallout protection (in the event prepared shelter might be unavailable, or too far away for you to go to):

1. A basement is usually better than aboveground floors, particularly in private residences. (In large commercial or civic buildings, however, the central areas of middle floors offer good protection.)

2. A corner of a basement that is below ground level is better than the center of the basement.

3. On aboveground floors, an improvised shelter should be situated away from outside walls.

4. A small, improvised shelter can provide some protection. The shielding mass should be concentrated immediately around and above the occupant to conserve construction time.

5. Stay away from windows and outside doorways, because these are weak points in the fallout shield. Also, windows could be shattered, even though located many miles beyond the severe blast damage area of a nuclear explosion.

6. If caught out in the open, try to get to some substantial structure such as a large commercial or civic building, a tunnel, or cave. If none of these is readily available, look for a culvert, underpass, or ditch—anything that will permit concealment below ground level—and improvise a shelter.

CHAPTER 6

COMMUNITY SHELTER PLANNING

Purpose of Community Shelter Planning

The community shelter plan is *the foundation of local emergency readiness.*

A substantial inventory of fallout shelter has been identified in the United States, and the Department of Defense shelter program is making orderly progress toward the goal of shelter for each citizen, so located as to be available where needed, whether near his home, school, place of work, or elsewhere.

If an attack were to occur in the near future, the shelter already identified and marked could save many lives. This is because people who were in buildings affording shelter, or who were nearby and knew that the shelter signs identified protected areas, would know where to go. However, neither the shelters now marked nor those which will be added in the future can function at maximum effectiveness until *every* citizen knows where to go and what to do in case of attack.

The next essential step in developing operational local civil defense systems is to build upon the investment represented by the shelter program by determining what each citizen should do in time of emergency and by *getting that information to the individual.* The largest part of this job involves matching the people in small geographic areas to the best protected space now available, and making these allocations known. Shelter deficit areas must also be defined with precision, so that efforts to identify or create more shelter can be focused in these areas.

In addition, existing local emergency plans must be updated to base them on shelter allocation plans—thus creating a working, shelter-based local civil defense system. This includes, for example, detailed local preparations for managing law and order problems associated with sheltering the population, for manning shelters with shelter managers and radiation monitors, for communications between shelters and emergency operating centers, and for support by available military units.

Concept of Community Shelter Planning

Community shelter planning enables a local government to give its people information so they may answer the questions, "Where do

I go?" and "What do I do?" in case of nuclear attack. The plan does this by allocating public shelters to be used by people located in specific areas of the community, thus assuring the best use of the best existing protected space. The public is informed of these allocations through public news media and other means—including maps showing shelter locations. (Allocation plans must be updated as new shelter space is identified or created and as population patterns change.) The community shelter plan includes information for those people for whom public shelter is not now available; for example, instructions on how to improve the protection existing in homes, including action which can be taken to do this in a crisis period.

The community shelter plan also defines precisely areas of shelter deficit within the community. This allows concrete and specific local procedures to be established to alleviate deficits, by applying funds and effort where they are needed under programs to identify shelter in smaller structures, to provide packaged ventilation kits to increase space usable in shelters already identified, and to provide professional advice on the use of newly developed techniques to incorporate shelter (at little or no cost) in the design of new buildings.

Finally, the community shelter plan provides for updating local civil defense emergency plans, to base them upon the shelter allocation plan developed by the community shelter planning project.

National Community Shelter Planning Program

Experience in community shelter planning field-test projects to date has shown that developing shelter allocation plans is an activity which professional city planners are best equipped to handle, just as architects and engineers are best able to survey buildings for fallout protection. Accordingly, the Office of Civil Defense will provide the services of urban planning professionals to communities developing community shelter plans.

In localities where the size and complexity of the job—which depends primarily on the size of the locality and the amount of shelter available—requires work by on-site local urban planners, the Office of Civil Defense is presently funding this work directly. This is being done by means of a contract between the locality and the appropriate U.S. Army Corps of Engineers or U.S. Navy Facilities Engineering Command district office. Professional urban planner assistance for other areas will be provided by an Office of Civil Defense-funded "State Community Shelter Planning Officer," who is an employee of the State.

Description of the Community Shelter Plan

All community shelter plans developed under the National Community Shelter Planning Program will include the six steps described below:

Step I—Current shelter capability allocation plan

The Step I allocation plan is required to make use of the shelter capability of the community; that is, the *best protected space currently available,* in order to provide the best protection possible for the entire population. This includes the use, where and as necessary, of all space located by the National Fallout Shelter Survey and the Smaller Structures Survey, as well as making the best arrangements possible for those people for whom public shelter is not now available.

Surveyed shelters with a protection factor less than 40 will be used temporarily where and as necessary. Departure from the 10 square foot space-per-person planning factor, where feasible, and movement times exceeding planning estimates of 30 minutes in urban and suburban areas and 60 minutes in rural areas, by a reasonable amount will be employed as necessary to make maximum use of all surveyed space—to use available public shelter to accommodate as much of the population as possible.

In areas where there is not sufficient public shelter for all of the population, the amount of shelter identified in homes will be considered in calculating the number of people for whom public shelter is needed. Any arrangements for the use by neighbors of shelter identified in homes should be based on voluntary and spontaneous action by citizens. The Office of Civil Defense does not require or recommend that local governments encourage or foster such cooperative neighborhood arrangements. This is based on the premise that use of shelter space identified in homes by persons other than the residents must be a matter of individual option by the householder who has the shelter space available, and that such use must be at his initiative.

Step I allocation plans will provide, where necessary, for vehicular movement utilizing available automobiles and buses for the best use of available public shelter. This does not involve a massive movement of people from outlying areas or suburbs to central business districts of cities. Rather, vehicular movements will be planned over relatively short distances and for specified areas only, for the best possible use of available shelter.

In the absence of better protection, people for whom public shelter is not now available, or who cannot be accommodated in shelter of known protection factor identified in homes, will be advised to seek shelter in the best-protected parts of their homes, whether or not the homes have basements. They will be provided instructions, based on community shelter plan Step II work, on how to improve the protection afforded by their homes. (See Ch. 5.)

As new shelter is added to the local inventory and as allocation plans are updated, public shelter space not meeting criteria for marking and stocking as public shelters will be phased out of the local community shelter plan. Thus, the allocation plan eventually will be based on the use of space with protection factors of 40 or better, of rated capacity, and on movement times of 30 minutes in urban and suburban areas and 60 minutes in rural areas.

Step II—Emergency information readiness

Step II of community shelter planning requires that the local government be prepared to advise the people on where to go and what to do in case of nuclear attack. This includes information on the location of all available public shelters, and on routes to take to these shelters, as well as information for people for whom there is no public shelter available under the Step I plan; for example, on how to improve the fallout protection afforded by their homes.

During Step II, localities will prepare detailed plans both for disseminating community shelter planning information to the public soon after the community shelter plan is approved by the local government and the Office of Civil Defense, and for disseminating similar advice in periods of increased international tension. The information prepared in Step II for later dissemination to the public will be in the form of maps and recommended emergency actions.

Step III—Identification of shelter deficits

The purpose of Step III is to identify shelter deficits on a uniform basis throughout the country, by quantity and by geographical location. Step III results will also form the basis for local work on Step IV, procedures for development of shelter.

Step III requires identifying and defining with precision local deficits of shelter meeting Office of Civil Defense minimum criteria (i.e., protection factor 40 or better, 10 sq. ft. of ventilated space or 500 cu. ft. of unventilated space per person), using standard criteria for movement time (30 mins. in urban or suburban areas, 60 mins. in rural areas). This includes both present deficits and anticipated future deficits, taking into consideration shelter expected to be added by new construction or subtracted by demolition, as well as population change predicted in local urban planning.

Step IV—Procedures for development of shelter

Step IV includes both immediate and long-term local government action to alleviate the present and anticipated future shelter deficits identified in Step III, using all means available or which may become available.

The immediate action is to prepare a plan for the use of packaged ventilation kits, based on the use of all ventilable space in the community shelter planning area which is needed. When kits are delivered, the packaged ventilation kit plan can be used as one of the bases for updating the Step I shelter capability allocation plan.

The long-term program calls for specific local government procedures that will encourage incorporation of shelter in new public and private buildings constructed in shelter-deficit areas. Specific responsibilities are assigned to local government agencies and departments, and a recommended local ordinance on incorporating shelter in new public buildings is prepared.

The long-term program also includes plans for making full use of assistance offered under the Office of Civil Defense Professional Development Services, to ensure that newly developed design techniques for incorporating fallout shelter at little or no cost are considered in the design of new buildings, both public and private, in shelter-deficit areas. With respect to public buildings, the recommended ordinance will have the effect of requiring that these techniques be considered. With respect to private structures, architects and engineers designing the buildings will be contacted and advised on the use of the new techniques. Owners should also be contacted.

Step IV will also detail local programs to attempt to meet remaining deficits. These may include, especially in rural areas, a program to promote home shelter construction.

Finally, Step IV includes details on procedures for updating the Step I shelter capability allocation plan, with updating responsibilities assigned to specific local government agencies, (e.g., the city planning department, city engineer, or civil defense coordinating staff).

Step V—Directive(s) for updating local civil defense emergency plans

Step V requires the community shelter planning project staff to prepare a directive(s) for updating local civil defense emergency plans, to base them on the Step I shelter allocation plan. The purpose is to develop the local capability needed to make the shelter allocation plan work. In other words, the updated civil defense plan, based on the community shelter planning shelter allocation plan, states how the local government will operate in emergency to protect its citizens, using the best fallout protection available locally.

The functional areas to be covered by the Step V directive include warning, shelter organization and staffing, radiological defense, fire services, maintenance of law and order, communications, emergency operating center staffing and procedures, Emergency Broadcast System, military support, increased readiness measures, emergency health and welfare services, and others as required.

Step VI—Official adoption or approval of community shelter plan

Step VI requires local official consideration of Steps I to V, resulting in whatever local legislative or executive action is required under State statute or local ordinance officially to adopt or approve the community shelter plan.

CHAPTER 7

PREPARING FOR EMERGENCY OPERATIONS

All actions in civil defense are in preparation for emergency operations. This is the meaning of civil defense: civil government, industry, and the public prepared for effective action in time of disaster.

Certainly, the preparation of a nationwide fallout shelter system is the key element of civil defense emergency operations. The reason fallout shelter is discussed in this book is that it has lifesaving capability by itself and is essential to the feasibility of all other civil defense preparations in the damage-limiting systems of national defense. All other civil defense emergency operations are secondary to the shelter system, and are in support of it. Development of civil defense capability automatically increases community effectiveness in handling lesser emergencies.

WARNING

One of the essential supporting systems is the warning system. For people to receive the maximum benefit from the fallout shelter system, they must receive timely warning of attack so that they can move to the best available fallout protection before fallout arrives. A Defense Department study on this subject indicates that the difference between having an effective warning system or not could mean the saving of an additional 2 to 8 percent of the preattack population—depending on the type and severity of the attack and other factors. This represents a saving of something like 4 to 15 million lives as a result of people being able to take timely survival actions based on the local community shelter plan.

The present Civil Defense Warning System is a combination of Federal, State, and local systems. The Federal portion of the system is termed the National Warning System (NAWAS). This system is essentially an extension of the military warning and detection systems that feed into the Combat Operations Center of the North American Air Defense Command (NORAD) at Colorado Springs, Colorado. Segments of NAWAS have also been used for severe weather warnings.

North American Air Defense Command

The North American Air Defense Command—a joint United States-Canadian defense system—maintains a surveillance network that includes ground radar installations and radar-equipped aircraft across the northern reaches of North America. Far to the north, lines of detection stations face the North Pole, Europe, Russia, and Asia. Other radar-equipped planes are on duty off our shores watching and listening for danger that might be approaching across the Atlantic or Pacific.

The capability to detect attacking aircraft begins at the Distant Early Warning Line (DEW Line), a radar chain extending some 4,000 miles across the Arctic, through the Bering Sea, and into the North Pacific. Navy and Air Force long-range, radar-equipped patrol planes extend the Distant Early Warning Line far out to sea. Farther south is the Mid-Canada Radar Line and the contiguous radars of the United States and Canada.

Ballistic Missile Early Warning System

The U.S. Air Force operates a system of giant radar installations that can spot intercontinental ballistic missiles (ICBMs) thousands of miles across the Arctic. This system, called the Ballistic Missile Early Warning System (BMEWS), is especially designed to warn of approaching intercontinental missiles. The Ballistic Missile Early Warning System installations are located at Thule, Greenland; Clear, Alaska; and Fylingdales Moor, England. Ballistic Missile Early Warning System reports can establish (1) that missiles have been fired, (2) the areas from which they were fired, and (3) the very general area of North America where missiles are expected to land. In a matter of seconds, electronic computers analyze the signals, compute data, and transmit findings to the North American Air Defense Command. (See fig. 34.)

National Warning System

The backbone of the Civil Defense Warning System is the National Warning System (NAWAS). This system consists principally of three major Office of Civil Defense Warning Centers (one at the North American Air Defense Command Combat Operations Center; one at an Office of Civil Defense Regional Headquarters; and one in the Washington, D.C. area) ; plus backup centers at the other Office of Civil Defense regional headquarters, which are linked by a special voice communications system to more than 700 warning points located in key facilities and population centers throughout the Nation. These warning points, manned on a 24-hour basis, are located at State police, local police and fire dispatching headquarters, and similar emergency facilities —including key Federal installations. Through a relay system, these warning points send warning information to local authorities who are responsible for sounding public warning devices, such

FIGURE 34.—A Ballistic Missile Early Warning System site.

as sirens. Figure 35 illustrates the association of warning network elements.

Warning Signals

The principal means of warning the public is the outdoor attack warning siren system. In some areas, horns, whistles, or other devices are used for the same purpose. Everyone should be familiar with the signals used on the public warning system and know what to do when the signals are sounded. (See fig. 36.)

Attack Warning Signal

The Attack Warning Signal is a 3- to 5-minute wavering tone on sirens, or series of short blasts on horns or other devices—repeated as necessary. This signal means that an actual attack against the United States has been detected and that *immediate protective action should be taken.* As a matter of national civil defense policy, the attack warning signal is used for no other purpose and has no other meaning.

Attention or Alert Signal

Public warning devices may be used to get public attention in emergencies. The signal is known as the Attention or Alert Signal (either or both). The signal is a 3- to 5-minute steady

THE WARNING NETWORK

Here's what would happen if an enemy air attack were launched against our continent:

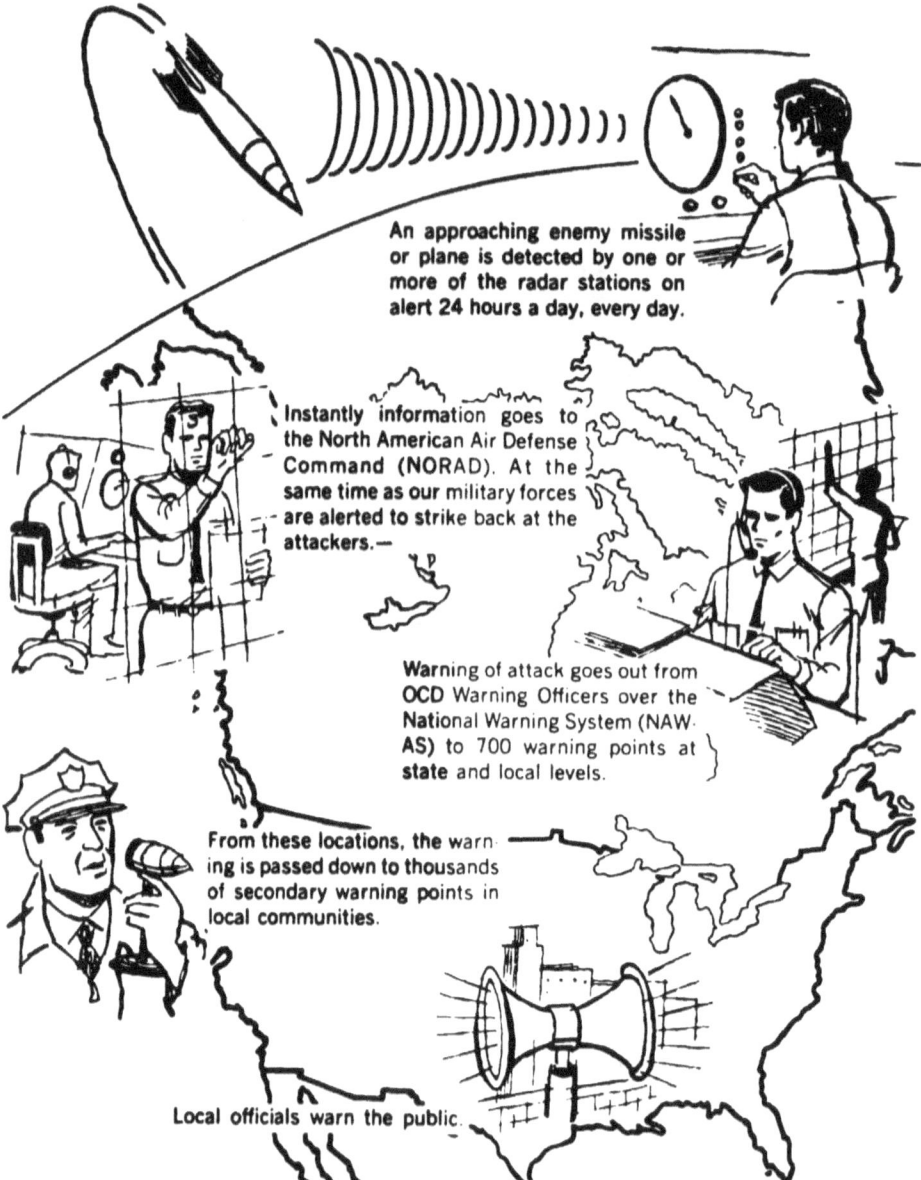

An approaching enemy missile or plane is detected by one or more of the radar stations on alert 24 hours a day, every day.

Instantly information goes to the North American Air Defense Command (NORAD). At the same time as our military forces are alerted to strike back at the attackers.

Warning of attack goes out from OCD Warning Officers over the National Warning System (NAWAS) to 700 warning points at state and local levels.

From these locations, the warning is passed down to thousands of secondary warning points in local communities.

Local officials warn the public.

FIGURE 35.—Association of warning network elements.

tone. It may be sounded at the option and on the authority of local government officials. They will determine the circumstances under which the signal is to be activated (including whether or not it is

THE ATTACK WARNING SIGNAL

A WAVERING TONE OR SHORT BLASTS FOR 3 TO 5 MINUTES
ACTUAL ATTACK AGAINST THIS COUNTRY HAS BEEN DETECTED --
TAKE IMMEDIATE PROTECTIVE ACTION.

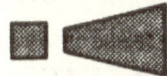

THE ATTENTION OR ALERT SIGNAL

A STEADY BLAST OR TONE FOR 3 TO 5 MINUTES --
LISTEN FOR ESSENTIAL EMERGENCY INFORMATION !

FIGURE 36.—Warning signals: Attack Warning; and Attention or Alert Signal.

to be used for warning of natural disasters). In addition to any other meaning or requirement for action as determined by local government officials, the signal means to all persons in the United States—"Listen for essential emergency information."

The *outdoor* public alerting system is limited in its effectiveness, and for several years studies have been conducted to develop a practical *indoor* warning system. The discontinuance of CONELRAD restrictions on radio broadcasting in time of national emergency has opened explorations of radio warning systems as highly attractive avenues for the improvement of warning capability.

COORDINATION OF ACTION

Much of civil defense emergency operations is concerned with the processing of information—gathering information on the extent of the emergency and the damage caused, and transmitting directions and guidance so that those who are responsible for recovery actions can operate effectively.

Coordinating this flow of essential emergency information and guidance is a primary responsibility of the executive head of a government unit, assisted by his civil defense director and other key government officials. To carry out this job, they need a protected communication headquarters from which to operate. The Office of Civil Defense assists State and local governments in developing these emergency headquarters—usually termed "emergency operating centers"—by matching funds for the development of centers and necessary emergency communications equipment which meet Office of Civil Defense standards. By the end of December 1965, the Office of Civil Defense had matched funds for 707 emergency operating centers of State and local governments.

Operational Communications

The primary network for carrying Federal-State civil defense operational information is the Civil Defense Communications System No. 1 (NACOM 1), which consists of a leased teletypewriter network with alternate telephone facilities. The Civil Defense Communications System No. 1 connects the Office of Civil Defense national and regional offices, State civil defense offices, and the national emergency relocation sites of selected Federal agencies; and interconnects with commercial, military, and other government teletypewriter communications systems.

As a backup to NACOM 1, the Office of Civil Defense is developing Civil Defense Communications System No. 2 (NACOM 2) which is a high-frequency radio network using voice, radiotelegraph, and radio-teletype transmissions. At the beginning of 1965, NACOM 2 installations were completed to link Office of Civil Defense regions with about half the States, plus Puerto Rico and the Canal Zone.

Shelter Communications

In a civil defense emergency, communications would be necessary between public fallout shelters, to shelter control points, and the local emergency operating center. Each EOC would transmit directions and information to shelters within its area. Telephone service and the Emergency Broadcast System are the primary means of shelter communications. Within some large shelters, information and instructions to occupants might be provided by public address systems.

Communications with the Public

Getting official information and guidance to the public in time of national emergency could be directly responsible for saving millions of lives. An Emergency Broadcast System (EBS) has been established to provide the President and the Federal Government, and State and local governments, with a means of communicating with the public through commercial broadcast stations in the period preceding, during, and following an enemy attack.

An Emergency Broadcast System plan, effective January 6, 1964, was developed in accordance with Executive Order 11092 of February 26, 1963, assigning certain emergency preparedness functions to the Federal Communications Commission. Management of the Emergency Broadcast System is primarily a responsibility of the Federal Communications Commission, and the plan for its operation is based upon requirements of the White House, the Office of Emergency Planning, and the Office of Civil Defense.

Upon implementation of the Emergency Broadcast System plan in a national emergency, those commercial broadcasting stations holding National Defense Emergency Authorizations issued by the Federal Communications Commission will remain on the air at their regular broadcasting frequencies to transmit official information and instructions. All other broadcasting stations will leave the air.

The Office of Civil Defense is working closely with the Federal Communications Commission and the broadcast industry to assure that major Emergency Broadcast System stations could continue to operate in a fallout environment following a nuclear attack. The U.S. Army Corps of Engineers and the U.S. Navy Facilities and Engineering Command, through contracts with broadcast stations, are carrying out a Civil Defense Broadcast Station Protection Program, for the Office of Civil Defense. The program consists of three main parts:

1. *Fallout protection* at broadcast transmitting sites to protect the people needed to operate the stations.
2. *Emergency power* to provide the stations with a capability to continue operation if normal power is disrupted.
3. *Radio program links* and associated equipment needed to transmit local, State, and regional programing from the seats of government to Emergency Broadcast System stations for transmission to the public.

As of January 1, 1966, a total of 531 Emergency Broadcast System stations were a part of this Office of Civil Defense protection program. The intent is to extend the program to 658 Emergency Broadcast System stations.

The type of information that would go out over the Emergency Broadcast System and other information media in time of national emergency, and the manner in which it would be disseminated, is a vital part of the public information planning mission. Getting basic civil defense instructions to the public in time of crisis could save many lives in event of an attack. At the same time, any system for emergency public information must not act to increase the crisis level nor hamper the President in his efforts to resolve the emergency.

RADIOLOGICAL MONITORING

After a nuclear attack, information on radioactive fallout would be critical to survival and recovery actions. Every level of government would need a capability for measuring and evaluating postattack fallout conditions so that government officials could make sound decisions affecting: (1) the period of shelter occupancy; (2) restoration of vital facilities and services, and obtaining needed food, water, and other supplies at the earliest possible time;

(3) firefighting, law-enforcement, and other public safety operations; (4) relocation of people from areas of high radiation intensity; (5) rescue, first aid, medical, and welfare operations; (6) decontamination and other recovery and rehabilitation operations; and (7) control of radiation exposures of workers assigned to emergency recovery tasks in fallout areas.

To obtain adequate coverage for civilian units of government, the Office of Civil Defense estimates that a large number of radiological monitoring stations will have to be established throughout the Nation. Many of these will be located in public fallout shelters. Others must be located at Federal, State, and local governmental facilities. For every monitoring station meeting Office of Civil Defense criteria, including a minimum of two trained monitors and suitable communications, the Office of Civil Defense provides at least one set of radiological defense operational instruments consisting of three survey meters, two dosimeters, and a dosimeter charger.

As of February 1, 1966, there was a total of 56,715 stations in the civilian radiological monitoring system, including 10,206 in Federal facilities and 46,509 in State and local facilities. In addition, 79,868 monitoring instrument kits had been supplied to 73,969 public fallout shelters.

MILITARY SUPPORT OF CIVIL DEFENSE

Military forces are in a position to render valuable assistance to civil authorities in the event of a nuclear attack, and troops are receiving appropriate training. Under a plan which has been approved by all the State Governors, the State Adjutants General and their headquarters will be used to plan for military support of civil defense and to direct military forces committed within the State for civil defense assistance in the event of a nuclear attack.

Under the plan, the State Adjutant General and the State military headquarters would be brought into Federal active service in the event of a nuclear attack. The State Adjutant General would then be under the command of the continental United States Army Commander in whose area he is located, and would command the military support forces within his State which are made available for the military support mission.

The plan affects the 48 continental States and the District of Columbia. Since the military organizations in Alaska and the overseas areas, including Hawaii, are under the armed services unified commanders, provision of instructions for military support of civil defense in these areas is a responsibility of the Joint Chiefs of Staff.

During the pre-mobilization phase, the Governor of each State, through his Adjutant General, would have necessary control of planning which affects his State. After mobilization a familiar means of coordination would exist between the Governor and the senior military authority responsible for military support to the State government civil defense operations.

The plan provides a military chain of command, paralleling the civil government structure, to improve the effectiveness of military cooperation with State authorities. In an attack emergency, local requirements would be assessed and conveyed by the Governor or his civil defense director to the State military commander who would employ the military resources within the State, active and reserve, which are made available to him for military support of civil defense.

The plan in no way assigns civil defense to the military. Strong as they are, the military forces represent only a small percentage of United States manpower and equipment potential. Not only would it be physically impossible for the military to take over the responsibility for civil defense across the Nation, but it would also conflict with the primary responsibility of the Armed Forces to carry out their military mission. The role of the military in civil defense is to assist and support civil authority.

TRAINING

Preparation for effective action in time of emergency requires training. The Office of Civil Defense conducts or sponsors a variety of training programs, as detailed below.

Civil Defense University Extension Program

Civil Defense Conferences are primarily designed to review with State, county, and municipal government officials their civil defense emergency and disaster responsibilities, and to encourage continual improvement in their capability to cope with emergency situations. Conferences provide further information concerning civil defense policies and programs, particularly the National Community Shelter Planning Program. These sessions do not exceed one day and are generally planned for the specific needs of the expected majority of the audience.

Shelter Management for Instructors Course prepares selected individuals as shelter management instructors. The course includes the methods, techniques, and procedures of planning, organizing, and conducting local shelter management training programs. Topics covered are management of public fallout shelters, with instruction on organization and staff requirements, supplies and equipment, shelter entry, operations and living, and emergence from shelter. A shelter exercise is included in the course.

Radiological Monitoring for Instructors Course qualifies selected individuals as radiological monitor instructors. The course covers basic concepts of nuclear science and nuclear weapons effects; types and operation of radiological defense equipment, and practical experience in using this equipment in radiation areas; formation, decay, and forecasting of radioactive fallout; protection against fallout; source-handling techniques; and monitoring operations.

Shelter Management Course trains individuals who may be needed to assist in the management of public fallout shelters. This course provides instruction in the duties of a shelter manager and staff assistants; includes shelter organization and operation, shelter entry, radiological defense measures, safety and maintenance, feeding, sleeping arrangements, health and sanitation, information and training within the shelter, and procedures in preparing to leave the shelter.

Civil Defense Management Course covers the basic functions and duties of the civil defense director, as well as the responsibilities of State and local officials in major subject areas. These areas include the national civil defense program, the effects of nuclear weapons, with particular attention to radiation and protection against it, local organization and staffing, the legal basis of civil defense, warning, communications and emergency operations, shelter requirements, public information, and training and education.

Radiological Defense Officer Course qualifies selected individuals as operations staff members in assembling, evaluating, coordinating, and disseminating radiological intelligence that will enable them to provide (1) technical guidance in radiological defense planning and operations, and (2) on-the-job staff training. The course includes instruction on the National Radiological Defense Program, radiological countermeasures, technical guidance for radiological defense planning and operations, direction and coordination of monitoring operations, reporting and control center procedures, and postattack recovery measures, including decontamination. Practical experience is given in the application of these concepts to emergency operations.

U. S. Office of Education, Civil Defense Adult Education Program

Personal and Family Survival Course (12 hours) is designed to develop an understanding of the role of the individual, family, and community in civil defense. The following topics represent the course content: the National Civil Defense Program, modern weapons and radioactive fallout, public fallout shelters, shelter occupancy, fallout protection at home, community shelter planning, emergence from shelters and recovery, and survival on the farm.

Radiological Monitoring Course (16 hours) prepares students to serve as radiological monitors on a shelter management staff or with an emergency operating crew (fig. 37). The course includes the following topics: nuclear weapons effects, with emphasis on fallout; practical use and simple maintenance of civil defense radiological instruments; effects of fallout and radiation exposure guidance; food, water, equipment and personnel decontamination; dose and dose-rate calculations; and local radiological defense operational procedures, including practical exercises in use of instruments.

FIGURE 37.—Radef monitors must be trained.

U. S. Public Health Service

Medical Self-Help Course (16 hours) is designed to provide knowledge and some skills in treating injuries and caring for the sick in case of a nuclear attack or any disaster. The techniques taught were selected on the assumption that a doctor or nurse might not be available for a relatively long period of time. The course includes the following topics: radioactive fallout and shelter, healthful living in emergencies, artificial respiration, bleeding and bandaging, fractures and splinting, transportation of the injured, burns, shock, nursing care of the sick and injured, infant and child care, and emergency childbirth.

U. S. Department of Agriculture

Rural Civil Defense Education Program is designed to inform and instruct rural families in measures of personal survival in time of nuclear attack and in the protection of their livestock, feed, water, and foodstuffs from radioactive fallout. Informational materials are readily available through the State Cooperative Extension Offices and county agents. The Rural Fallout Shelter Analysis Workshop is a 2-day training session for agricultural engineers. This includes discussion of shielding fundamentals, shielding calculations, and use of shielding analysis forms.

U. S. Continental Army Command

Radiological Monitoring (Contents of course the same as for the Radiological Monitoring course described above.)

Requests for training are directed through OCD Regional Offices to appropriate military channels.

Office of Civil Defense Staff College

The OCD Staff College at Battle Creek, Michigan, offers professional courses. All are 5-day courses, with classes beginning on Mondays. The following courses are currently scheduled:

> Civil Defense Management
> Radiological Monitoring for Instructors
> Shelter Management (Instructor)
> Radiological Defense Officer
> Civil Defense Planning and Operations I, II, III
> Advanced Civil Defense Management
> Industrial Civil Defense Management
> Seminars and Workshops

Civil Defense Professional Development Program

The Office of Civil Defense, through selected schools and departments of Architecture and Engineering at universities, offers special professional development courses in fallout shelter analysis and design to architects and engineers. These courses cover the techniques of evaluating fallout protection in existing buildings, and the application of "slanting" techniques to improve both the quantity and quality of fallout shelter in new or remodeled buildings. Advanced courses and seminars are held for those architects and engineers who have successfully completed the basic course.

For information concerning exact courses available, dates, and procedures for enrollment in these courses, contact your local or State civil defense office.

State and Local Training

State and local governments are conducting additional training courses to meet their identified needs for additional trained people to augment the existing personnel of their governmental staffs during emergencies.

RESEARCH AND DEVELOPMENT

Office of Civil Defense research is another major aspect of support to community shelter readiness. The Office of Civil Defense conducts a coordinated research effort to develop the best methods, materials, and facilities for use by all levels of government in civil defense.

Most of the research effort is devoted to a "core program" of long-term nature to improve the state of knowledge in various technical areas. This effort is in the nature of an investment which may be expected to pay dividends in future years. In addition, the Office of Civil Defense directs a number of "output studies" each year to provide guidance for policy and operational decisions and to improve civil defense equipment.

During the 1965-66 period, research was being carried out in four major program areas:

1. *Shelter Research*—Emphasis on the means for providing fallout shelter space at minimum cost, methods of achieving a complete fallout shelter system, and potential methods of producing better shelter systems.
2. *Support Systems Research*—Emphasis on the means for minimizing the thermal and fire problem associated with nuclear attack, and on the development of improved methods for emergency operations.
3. *Postattack Research*—Emphasis on development of a firm technical basis for understanding the probable environment immediately after an attack and on methods to reduce hazards to life in the period when people would be able to leave fallout shelter.
4. *Systems Evaluation Research*—Emphasis on development of improved methods for determining the probable cost, effectiveness, and feasibility of various civil defense programs.

Research is carried out under Office of Civil Defense direction by other Department of Defense and Federal agencies, by universities, and by private research organizations. At the beginning of 1965, the Office of Civil Defense had about 200 research contracts with more than 75 different organizations throughout the United States. Two laboratories—the U.S. Naval Radiological Defense Laboratory and the Stanford Research Institute—aid in the management and direction of these individual studies.

LIAISON WITH ORGANIZATIONS

Many nongovernmental organizations are in a position to assist and support local communities in preparing for effective emergency operations. The Office of Civil Defense provides informational guidance and other aids for these organizations to use in incorporating civil defense preparedness concepts and measures into their regular programs. This type of liaison covers a wide spectrum of national organizations in such areas as education, business and industry, labor, architecture and engineering, health and welfare, veterans, fraternal, civic affairs, and youth groups.

MANAGEMENT ASSISTANCE

Programs of Federal Matching Funds

As further support to community shelter readiness, the Office of Civil Defense administers a program of Federal matching funds to improve the emergency operational facilities, equipment, and staffs of State and local civil defense. This includes financial assistance to build emergency operating centers, purchase necessary equipment for warning and emergency communications, meet necessary administrative expenses, and send personnel to the Office of Civil Defense Staff College for civil defense training.

Civil defense facilities and equipment acquired under the matching funds program are intended for use in event of an attack on the United States or in preparation for such an emergency. In addition, the Office of Civil Defense has authorized the following other uses:

1. To combat or relieve the effects of disasters not resulting from enemy attack.
2. The general use of communications equipment, providing: (a) that such use does not involve removal of the equipment from its place of use for civil defense purposes, and (b) that such use does not jeopardize its immediate availability in operating condition for civil defense purposes.

As part of the civil defense financial assistance program, the Office of Civil Defense is supporting a management-assistance program aimed at improving the capability of civil defense staff personnel at State and local levels. The program is termed the Personnel and Administrative Expenses Program (frequently referred to as "the P and A program"). For those governmental units taking part in this program, the Office of Civil Defense matches funds for State and local civil defense personnel and administrative expenses. The personnel must be hired under an approved merit system.

In 1961, when the program began, 702 counties and municipalities took part in it. At the beginning of 1965, participation had grown to 1,435 counties and municipalities. The people residing in these communities represented more than 60 percent of the total United States population.

All 50 States, Puerto Rico, the Virgin Islands, Guam, American Samoa, and Washington, D. C., take part in the program. The number of State and local civil defense employees partially supported by this program has grown from 3,638 in 1961 to 5,302 at the beginning of 1965.

Annual Program Paper

All State and local governments taking part in Federal civil defense financial assistance programs submit a program paper each fiscal year. This is a management document which describes the specific things a State or local government intends to do during the fiscal year to build its civil defense capability. The program paper reports program goals, accomplishments to date, work remaining to be done, and how much of this remainder is programed for accomplishment in the fiscal year for which the program paper is submitted.

The Office of Civil Defense provides guidance for the preparation of these annual plans, which involves a number of decisions to achieve program balance between preparedness actions and the resources available to carry them out.

CHAPTER 8

EMERGENCE FROM SHELTERS AND RECOVERY

As radiation levels decay, it will be possible to schedule emergence from shelter. These plans and schedules will take into account the need for actions outside the shelter and the hazards presented by radiation. As it becomes possible to spend increasing periods of time outside shelter, the supply of food and other essentials to survival can be replenished, repairs and emergency restoration of public utilities and essential facilities begun, and actions leading to long-range national recovery undertaken.

WHEN TO LEAVE SHELTER

Within 24 hours after the end of the attack, nearly all the hazardous local fallout will be down on the ground, and radiological monitors will have determined how much fallout has occurred in each local area. It will then be possible for the radiological defense officers and monitors to make sufficiently accurate predictions of fallout radiation intensities to permit planning for emergence from shelter. Naturally, in those areas where the combination of actual attack pattern and meteorological conditions produced little or no fallout, people would come out of their shelters as soon as it could be known that the attack was over and there was no fallout problem in the area. In many areas, however, it would be necessary to wait until the radioactive materials in the fallout had decayed to acceptable levels.

The first trips outside shelter in these areas will probably be supervised by radiological monitors. Since radiation levels may vary from area to area, these monitors will measure radiation outside the shelter to ensure that it is within safe limits. Personnel radiation dosages should be limited by rotating assignment of people to make the trips. This will reduce the probability that any one person receives excessive exposure. (So far as possible, exposure of children and of adults not past child-bearing age should be avoided.)

In general, people should not expose themselves to radiation unless such action is essential for the welfare of shelter occupants or for the recovery of the community. Limited exposure may be justifiable when necessary for securing essential supplies, decontaminating needed facilities, repairing and rebuilding damaged essential structures, or evacuating a shelter during a sudden emergency. In these cases, the shelter manager must make the decision, based on a reasonable balance between a probable danger from exposure and the need to leave the shelter.

The shelter manager should be kept informed of the amounts of radiation exposure received by each occupant who goes outside shelter on brief, necessary trips, so that no individual or group receives an excessive amount.

In deciding whether to leave shelter temporarily or permanently, the general rule is that the longer the wait, the less the danger.

To minimize demands from occupants that shelter be vacated earlier than may be safe, the shelter manager and staff will need to find ways to make shelter living progressively less uncomfortable or more varied. Good light and reading materials, better food, recreation, and other conveniences will probably assume increasing importance as time goes on.

Where shelters are in large buildings, comfort might be increased by allowing some of the occupants to go to other floors or areas not designated as shelters, but still affording substantial protection when radiation levels decline somewhat.

If occupants are to remain in shelter for some time, the shelter staff must ensure that all understand why. The reasons will differ according to the local situation, but they should be clearly and honestly presented to the occupants.

People in home shelters should remain inside until assured by radio or other contact with local authorities that radiation has decayed to acceptable levels.

PRECAUTIONS WHEN LEAVING SHELTERS

In some areas, even when occupants are able to leave their shelters during the day, they may have to return to the shelters to sleep and eat. Their homes may have been destroyed or seriously damaged. High radiation levels may make it advisable to spend several hours behind shielding each day. These conditions could last for a considerable time. The shelter may, therefore, have to serve as a welfare center or as temporary housing for some occupants for several additional weeks or months.

Therefore, before permanently closing a public shelter, the shelter manager will have to be sure that all occupants are able to return to their homes or that satisfactory arrangements have been made for their assignment and transport to lodgings elsewhere. Plans for closing the shelters would be coordinated with the overall post-shelter emergency plans of the local government.

When survivors first emerge from shelters close to an attack area, they may find situations similar to those after a community has been struck by an earthquake or a hurricane. Most normal community services will have ceased. There may be the same danger of disease from disrupted sanitation systems and the same critical shortage of food and water, and need for information and medical help that exists after a natural disaster. Injured survivors may be seeking medical attention. Perhaps some will be emotionally disturbed. There may be a great deal of uncertainty and confusion.

Radioactive fallout could leave some areas or facilities close downwind of nuclear bursts contaminated for long periods of time. It may, therefore, be necessary in limited areas to relocate people for some time, and to provide lodging, food, and other necessities for them in other areas.

During the time the community is confined to shelters by high levels of radiation, it is possible that only temporary disposal can be made of human wastes, garbage, and other refuse. Now there will be a chance to dispose of it permanently through restoration of normal services or burial.

Waste disposal should be undertaken in conformity with local community ordinances, as reflected in civil defense emergency plans. It is probable that arrangements will be made to bury, burn, or dump wastes in selected locations. Careful attention should be given to this operation because improper disposal may cause disease, as well as the creation of a radiological hazard from the accumulation of fallout in a central place.

During this period of initial recovery, attention will be focused on local problems. Nearly everyone will need more food, water, and other vital supplies. Among the first steps in the local community's recovery effort will probably be the establishment of safe, uncontaminated areas where people can gather for organization into work groups. At this point, the community will again begin to function as a community.

An immediate problem will be to get agricultural activity back to normal, since the raising of food crops and livestock may be handicapped in some areas by high radiation levels. Chapter 9 deals with some of the special problems of farm communities after a nuclear attack.

DECONTAMINATION

Even after radiation has decayed enough to allow a return to near-normal community life, fallout might still be present in some areas to the extent that it would create a special hazard to health.

Decontamination of essential areas and facilities could make heavy demands upon manpower and other vital resources. In those areas where it would be feasible, trained manpower would be needed, and priorities would have to be set carefully. Work would have to be undertaken only on the projects most vital to the welfare of the community. Personal exposure of decontamination workers would have to be checked carefully on a continuing basis.

Plans for decontamination procedures involve use of high-pressure fire hoses and street flushers to clear paved or other hard-surface areas. Roofs might be decontaminated by using fire hoses; and unpaved areas by scraping off or plowing under the top layer of soil. Large earth-moving equipment could be used to do this. Another possible method of decontamination would be to cover a contaminated area with uncontaminated earth.

The radioactive materials that are gathered up might be flushed into storm drains or dumped into ditches and then be covered with earth. Materials might also be dumped in piles at safe distances from occupied areas. In all cases, decontamination does not destroy radiation; it only moves the source of radiation from a place where it is a hazard to essential operations to a position where it is not. The fallout particles may be physically moved or covered with earth or other shielding material.

SURVIVOR REGISTRATION AND INFORMATION

After emergence from shelter, everyone will undoubtedly want to obtain information and help. Such assistance will be available at the locations designated by local government. Everyone will want to find out about relatives and friends.

Among other forms that may be filled out during registration are a Post Office Safety Notification Form (fig. 38) and an Emergency Change of Address Form (fig. 39). These forms will help you to locate relatives and friends by mail, and to notify them of your safety.

FOOD, CLOTHING, AND HOUSING

Governments have plans to assure that all citizens get an equitable share of available resources and to meet vital community and individual requirements. The Emergency Welfare Services, U.S. Department of Health, Education, and Welfare—in coordination with the Office of Civil Defense—provides guidance to State and local governments on the welfare services that would be necessary in event of nuclear attack.

Public shelters might be kept open to provide housing for those people who are unable to return home because of destruction or

SAFETY NOTIFICATION CARD—NO POSTAGE REQUIRED

DIRECTIONS.—Fill in this card and mail it immediately after evacuation or attack to any person who might be concerned about your safety. Cards may be obtained free at Civil Defense registration points and Post Offices.

I AM / WE ARE SAFE AND CAN BE REACHED AT THIS ADDRESS UNTIL FURTHER NOTICE

(IF UNABLE TO GIVE DEFINITE MAIL ADDRESS SHOW "GENERAL DELIVERY")

(POST OFFICE) (STATE)

MEMBERS OF FAMILY INCLUDED IN THIS NOTIFICATION (IF NOT INDIVIDUAL SIGNER ONLY)

DATE ______ SIGNATURE ______

POD Form 810 (Feb. 1959) c60—16—74872-1 GPO

FIGURE 38.—Post Office Safety Notification Form.

PRINT ABOVE: (Last name) (First name) (Middle name or initial)	(Date prepared)
YOUR PRE-EMERGENCY ADDRESS (Print below)	YOUR PRESENT ADDRESS (Print below)
HOUSE NO. & STREET, OR BOX OR RURAL ROUTE NO.	If not definite; show "GENERAL DELIVERY"
CITY, ZONE NO., STATE	POST OFFICE - STATE
SIGN YOUR NAME BELOW	TITLE, IF AUTHORIZED AGENT

READ—IMPORTANT NOTICE

Complete and mail this card at once in order that the Post Office can locate you and forward your letter mail.

A SEPARATE LOCATOR CARD IS REQUIRED FOR EACH PERSON OR ESTABLISHMENT RECEIVING MAIL.

Submit a new card promptly every time you change your address. *NO POSTAGE REQUIRED.*

POD Form 809 Feb. 1959

MAIL FORWARDING ORDER
EMERGENCY CHANGE OF ADDRESS

FIGURE 39.—Post Office Emergency Change of Address Form.

high levels of radiation. Other survivors might choose to live with friends or relatives until it would be possible to return home or until other permanent arrangements could be made.

Food and water probably would be the greatest survivor need after people emerge from shelter. Supplies will be controlled and checked by local authorities. Survivors could be fed in large groups at feeding centers or be issued food rations, as appropriate.

After attack, open-water sources may be contaminated by germs from disrupted sewers as well as by fallout. Because such water sources will be important to survivors, local authorities will test them periodically, as usual, and will recommend any necessary action. Simple purification methods exist. Cloudy or unclear water should be strained through several thicknesses of paper towels or clean cloth, or else be allowed to settle in a deep container and then siphoned off. After that, water may be freed of germs with water purification tablets; or by boiling vigorously for a few minutes; or by adding 20 drops of iodine to a gallon of clear water or 40 drops to a gallon of cloudy water. Then it should be left to stand for 30 minutes. Liquid household bleaches of the sodium hypochlorite type can also be used. The label usually gives instructions.

Radiation itself does not affect water. It is only when radioactive particles get into the water that the water may be harmful. As discussed on page 32, compared to the hazard from external gamma radiation, contamination of food and water is a minor problem.

Food stored indoors should be safe to eat. This is especially true of food in freezers and refrigerators. Packaged foods, generally, will be edible if any fallout particles are removed from the package or can. It would be best to eat perishable foods first, especially if electricity and gas are cut off. Bread is still edible even when moldy; sour milk is drinkable. Fruits and vegetables with "rotten spots" cut out are safe to eat. If they have been exposed outdoors to fallout, they can be wiped, washed, or peeled.

EMERGENCY RESTORATION OF PUBLIC UTILITIES AND ESSENTIAL SERVICES

During the period of reconstruction, immediate attention will be devoted to restoring services needed for the establishment of vital community activities. The problems or tasks facing most communities may include establishment of food distribution systems, sanitation projects, restoration of public utilities, preservation of law and order, and preparation of casualty lists. Communities that are well organized to meet emergencies will better be able to meet these problems and recover in a shorter time than unorganized communities which have suffered like damage and receive similar outside aid.

SELF-SUFFICIENCY

All communities should plan to be self-reliant in the event of a nuclear attack. Many communities may be isolated—cut off from outside help, supplies, or information. Within a given area, it may be impossible to reach certain towns, villages, or even isolated houses. Surviving communities may be on their own for several weeks after the attack. It is quite possible that the roads, railroads, and bridges connecting one community with another, and with State and Federal Government centers may be destroyed or may have been made too dangerous to use by heavy concentrations of fallout. Aircraft may be needed elsewhere.

As a result, many areas might not receive from the rest of the Nation the immediate assistance they may have learned to expect after a localized natural disaster. When a hurricane, flood, or tornado strikes part of the Nation, unaffected communities can always be depended upon to rush assistance to the stricken areas. But all communities will be affected either directly or indirectly after a nuclear attack. Many communities will have serious recovery problems and will need additional supplies and manpower.

EMERGENCY REPAIRS

Some communities will experience blast damage to buildings, utilities, or transportation. Fires may add to the problem. In such circumstances, the community must determine how it can most effectively undertake emergency repairs when fallout radiation levels permit. In areas where buildings have been heavily damaged or destroyed, debris clearance will be a major operation. Plans must be made to undertake reconstruction efforts on the basis of priority survival and military needs.

If the community is faced with a shortage of surviving workers, a person may find it necessary to work temporarily at an unfamiliar job—a job which seems quite unsuitable to his particular abilities or knowledge. It is at a time like this that an individual will be called upon to put forth the best possible effort in whatever task must be done, until he can return to his normal occupation.

MUTUAL-AID PROGRAMS

Several States have organized intercounty and interstate plans to provide quick help in emergencies. These plans are designed so that, during the emergency repair and restoration period, support from outside can be sent without any legal or administrative complications. For example, New York, New Jersey, and Pennsylvania have agreements providing that, after a disaster, help can move swiftly and smoothly from one State to another. The plan fixes responsibility and makes unnecessary any special orders, signed documents, or new requisitions at the time of the disaster.

CIVIL DEFENSE IN INDUSTRY

In addition to planning for personal and family survival at home and in neighborhoods, it is important that civil defense plans be made at the workplace and in schools and other institutions.

The interest and concern of private industry in preparing for civil defense continues at a high level. Many companies have not only prepared for their own survival but are supporting and assisting local government in preparing for community survival.

Business and industrial establishments in general are capable of organizing for their own self-protection. Leadership is available, and employees can be organized and trained. In many cases, specialized equipment and supplies normally available can be used in emergency. Some form of emergency capability is already in existence in most industrial establishments; and this capability can be rapidly expanded or adapted in various ways to manage disaster conditions.

The workplace is one of the most effective channels for reaching people with civil defense preparedness information and guidance materials. Many companies have distributed CD publications and provided CD training for employees in methods of preparing for personal and family survival.

Recovery of the United States after a nuclear attack would depend in part on how thoroughly business and industrial enterprises have prepared to survive such an attack and resume production. Attention is being given, therefore, at all levels of government to programs that encourage the participation of business and industry in the civil defense planning of the communities in which their facilities are located. Industrial civil defense activities mean government-industry cooperation to (1) provide fallout shelter for employees and the public; (2) ensure on-premises warning in case of attack; (3) detect and report radioactive fallout hazards on the premises; and (4) organize and train employees in civil defense skills.

In addition to these basic elements of community civil defense planning, the managers of business and industrial establishments are encouraged to take protective action to provide for the continuity of corporate management and service to the public in the event of an enemy attack.

A few examples of the planning and cooperation that American business and industry have given in support of the National Civil Defense Program include:

1. More than 70 percent of the fallout shelters identified by the nationwide Fallout Shelter Survey are in buildings owned by business and industry. As of February 25, 1966, more than 105 thousand of the facilities owned by business and industry, containing in excess of 94 million shelter spaces, had been licensed and/or marked as public fallout shelters.
2. Shelters have been included in the design of many of the new buildings owned by business and industry. Many companies have spent their own funds to build fallout shelters for their

employees; existing structures have been modified by protective construction; and additional ventilation has been provided to create more habitable shelter space.

3. Some companies have purchased additional supplies and equipment to augment the austere survival supplies furnished by the Federal Government when a shelter is licensed for public use. Examples of such companies are: International Business Machines; Chase Manhattan Bank; Standard Oil Co. (New Jersey); Esso Research and Engineering Co.; The Deering Milliken Service Corp.; West Point Pepperell Manufacturing Co.; Boeing Co.; and dozens of others.

4. A great number of American business and industrial concerns have established corporate and plant industrial civil defense programs and have prepared and distributed civil defense manuals they have developed to assure uniformity of planning within their own corporations and plants. Among such companies are: Shell Oil; International Business Machines; Western Electric; Aetna Life Insurance; Radio Corporation of America; General Electric; Hughes Aircraft; International Harvester; Mobil Oil; General Motors; New York Telephone; and numerous others.

5. Recognizing the fact that knowledge backed by thoughtful planning is the key to survival in the Nuclear Age, many companies have taken advantage of courses offered by the Office of Civil Defense to train their employees in essential civil defense skills. More than 2,000 industrial executives have completed the one-week OCD Staff College course in "Industrial CD Management."

As a continuing activity, instructors who have been trained in other CD skills have returned to their companies to train others. Four thousand employees of the Detroit Edison Co. have been trained as radiological monitors. Originally, 100 of these employees were trained at OCD schools as radiological instructors; and they in turn trained other employees of the company. Three hundred employees were trained as shelter managers, and 9,000 employees have been scheduled for attendance at a new course in shelter occupancy, developed by the company. In addition, 1,700 employees have been scheduled to take the Medical Self-Help course administered by the U.S. Public Health Service. Some companies have trained all their employees in firefighting, rescue, and first aid. Among other companies that have on-going civil defense training for their employees are Jones and Laughlin Steel; Southern Bell Telephone; Mobil Oil; Western Electric; and Michigan Bell Telephone.

6. Informing and educating all employees about emergency planning for personal and family survival is another example of industry's cooperation with the national and local civil defense programs. In addition to CD publications which can be distributed at the workplace, company newsletters, magazines, bulletin boards, and other established communications media are all valuable in providing civil defense information to employees. Among the many companies that have established

such information programs are: Weyerhaeuser; Raytheon; Kimberly-Clark; Field Enterprises; The Chicago Sun Times and Daily News; Tidewater Oil; Radio Corporation of America; Eastman Kodak; Humble Oil; Ford Motor; and other companies previously mentioned.

Mutual Support Plans

Civil defense mutual support plans exist between many business and industrial firms and the local government serving their plant or office locations. Few companies are likely to have on hand, in the course of their normal operations, all of the facilities and equipment needed to deal with a major disaster. By organizing for mutual aid, industrial plants help each other and the local government with men and equipment when disaster strikes.

Under such a mutual-aid agreement, the participating companies agree to pool or exchange emergency equipment, manpower, or supplies in an orderly and planned fashion when a major disaster occurs. One member may be able to make available protected space for fallout shelter; another may be able to provide shelter supplies or equipment; and others may provide for communications, radiological monitoring, emergency medical care, etc.

The plant emergency and protective organization structure is quite similar to the protective organization structure of local governments. By augmenting appropriate departments of local government, organizational capability is achieved for managing communitywide disaster.

Industrial CD Checklist

Steps which should be taken by business, industrial, and commercial firms in preparing for civil defense at the workplace are presented in the checklist on the opposite page. Employees attending the Personal and Family Survival course should bring this checklist to the attention of their employers.

Most business and industrial leaders feel that civil defense preparedness is sound business practice. Such preparedness provides a kind of insurance for corporate survival in event of nuclear attack; and would be a vital element in survival of the United States as a free Nation.

A CHECKLIST OF PROCEDURES IN PREPARING FOR CIVIL DEFENSE IN INDUSTRY

1. Get in touch with your local civil defense director.
2. Appoint corporate and plant civil defense coordinators.
3. Select corporate and plant civil defense advisory committees.
4. Issue corporate policy directives establishing the civil defense program.
5. Train civil defense coordinators and committees at OCD Staff College.
6. Assess vulnerability of plant and corporate headquarters locations.
7. Arrange for receipt and dissemination of warning.
8. Establish a control center and communications system.
9. Develop emergency shutdown procedures.
10. Provide fallout shelter for employees and the public.
11. Plan for mass movement of employees to shelter.
12. Enlarge existing protective groups.
13. Organize employees into special groups for self-help.
14. Enroll these groups into departments of local government as auxiliaries.
15. Train for: shelter management, radiological monitoring, first aid and medical self-help, decontamination, rescue, firefighting.
16. Join with neighboring plants in organizing industrial mutual-aid associations.
17. Establish a security system for protection against espionage and sabotage.
18. Prepare to detect and report unexploded ordnance and unconventional weapons.
19. Establish executive succession list to ensure continuity of management.
20. Amend corporate bylaws and regulations as necessary.
21. Establish emergency corporate headquarters at alternate locations.
22. Protect vital company records and documents.
23. Plan for continuity of each important company function.
24. Assign emergency duties to department heads and appropriate employees.
25. Develop emergency financial procedures.
26. Designate postattack assembly points for employees.
27. Prepare to assess and report damage quickly following attack.
28. Plan for emergency repair and restoration.
29. Develop plans for quickly training employees following attack.
30. Deconcentrate production of critical items.
31. Disperse new industrial plants.
32. Prepare a manual of company and plant civil defense plans.
33. Tell employees about the company civil defense plan.
34. Test the disaster control plan with drills and exercises.
35. Inform and educate employees in methods of personal and home survival.
36. Publish civil defense information in company and employee publications.
37. Urge discussion of civil defense at employee meetings.
38. Tell stockholders about your company civil defense plan.
39. Let the public know that your company has prepared for civil defense.
40. Provide leadership, support, and assistance to local government in preparing for community survival.

OFFICE OF EMERGENCY PLANNING

The Office of Emergency Planning came into being September 22, 1961, to advise and assist the President in the total nonmilitary defense program of the United States. It is a staff arm of the President, as distinguished from the Office of Civil Defense, which is an operational arm.

The Director of the Office of Emergency Planning is appointed by the President and approved by the Senate. He is a statutory member of the National Security Council. National Headquarters for the Office of Emergency Planning is located in the Executive Office of the President, Washington, D.C.

There are eight OEP regional offices throughout the country to maintain liaison with State and local governments and with field offices of other Federal agencies. These regional offices are in the same locations and serve the same groups of States as the regional offices of the Office of Civil Defense.

Management of Resources

The very essential function of Emergency Management of Resources has no peacetime counterpart. Therefore, special planning arrangements are necessary. In time of emergency, an Office of Defense Resources will be established to perform this function.

The Office of Defense Resources will operate, on behalf of the President, at the apex of a Governmentwide resources management structure, in which the Federal agencies would be responsible for carrying out their assigned responsibilities. The Office of Defense Resources will be responsible for reviewing claims for resources and estimates of resources availability, and for advising the President with respect to feasible courses of action.

Staff members and Executive Reservists of the Office of Emergency Planning will provide the nucleus of the Office of Defense Resources. The work involved in the development of the Office of Defense Resources organizational structure will be done by the Office of Emergency Planning. When, and if, an emergency arises which necessitates activation of the Office of Defense Resources, the Office of Emergency Planning staff will be transferred immediately to the new Office, and the Director of the then operational Office of Defense Resources will report directly to the President. The Office of Defense Resources would be responsible for coordination and direction of resource management actions of the Federal Government, operating both at the national level and through eight regional offices.

The Director of the Office of Emergency Planning coordinates and directs the development and establishment of policies and plans for the mobilization and management of the Nation's resources and production. This includes such areas as food and water, economic stabilization, manpower, materials, industrial capacity, production facilities and equipment, construction, fuels and energy, and transportation.

The Director of the Office of Emergency Planning determines the kinds, forms, and quantities of strategic materials to be acquired or disposed of; and the objectives which govern the quantities of such materials to be held as a strategic reserve.

The present stockpiling law, the Strategic and Critical Materials Stock Piling Act, was passed in 1946. Incentives to encourage expansion of capacity and output in defense industries were incorporated in the Defense Production Act of 1950.

The Federal Government also maintains a Supplemental Stockpile of products acquired by the U.S. Department of Agriculture in exchange for surplus agricultural commodities.

Another inventory, acquired by the Department of Agriculture in exchange for surplus agricultural commodities, is held under the Commodity Credit Corporation account. These materials are for the immediate use of Government agencies and departments. If not consumed in this way, they must be transferred to the Supplemental Stockpile.

The Comprehensive Program

The Office of Emergency Planning has developed a "Comprehensive Program for Survival of Government and Management of Resources" which is now being extended to the State and local level. It is based on a concept of (1) the primacy of the war powers of the Federal Government, and (2) a need for a working partnership between Government and community leaders at all levels to achieve national preparedness.

In the event of nuclear attack, the people would look to government, not only to maintain law and order but to conserve and use surviving resources wisely.

Although it is unlikely that local communities would be "cut off" from national assistance and guidance for a protracted period, immediate action at the State level on economic resource problems solved in previous wars by the Federal Government would be required. In taking such action, State and local governments will carry out Federal as well as State laws to achieve national objectives. In such cases, Federal direction and control will be reestablished as soon as possible.

Emergency planning objectives include capability to:
1. Continue the services and functions of civil government.
2. Manage and provide essential resources—including food, fuel, power, transportation, and communications.

3. Control and preserve monetary and credit systems until Federal control can be reestablished.
4. Administer a consumer rationing system and other measures for the distribution of essential items for consumers.
5. Maintain a viable basic economic system to contribute to survival and recovery.

The Office of Emergency Planning is supporting, by contracts with State governments, emergency planning work at State level to accomplish these objectives.

Telecommunications

An Assistant Director of the Office of Emergency Planning has been designated as the Director of Telecommunications Management. He guides and encourages planning and preparedness efforts to help the Nation use telecommunications resources wisely in time of emergency.

The Executive Reserve

In 1955, an amendment to the Defense Production Act authorized the President to establish an executive reserve and to train executive reservists for employment in the Government in times of emergency. It had become increasingly evident that effective use of executive civilian talent is a keystone for the successful mobilization of our resources when the Nation is confronted by crisis. Therefore, in 1956, the President issued Executive Order 10660 establishing the National Defense Executive Reserve.

The Office of Emergency Planning coordinates the Reserve Program on behalf of the President.

CHAPTER 9

SURVIVAL ON THE FARM

In chapter 1, we saw that dangerous amounts of radiological fallout could occur anywhere in the Nation in event of attack. Hence, no farm or ranch is safe from the threat of fallout.

The problems of survival on the farm are, in many ways, more complex than those faced by a city or town resident. The urban dweller is individually responsible for some protective measures, but relies on his local government and his employer to supply part of the protection for him and his family by marking and stocking public shelter areas. Farmers and their families must necessarily undertake a much larger part of the protection of themselves and their means of livelihood.

In the event of an attack on this country, it is important to the welfare of the Nation that industry and business be protected to the extent possible in order that essential production be quickly reestablished. Likewise, it is essential not only that farmers and their families survive, but also that preparation be made to continue production of food and other necessary agricultural products. For these reasons, this chapter discusses both the measures for protection of the farm population, and measures that would help the farmer continue food production.

Many of the planned measures and procedures cannot be described adequately here. However, it is important for all of us to know that the continuing production of food, following an attack, is a most important part of civil defense preparations. By Executive Order, the President of the United States has given the U.S. Department of Agriculture (USDA) definite responsibilities for the protection of food and agriculture against effects of a nuclear attack. The USDA has developed guides for agricultural leaders and farmers. Also, USDA representatives in each county, working with local civil defense officials, are responsible following an attack for applying guidance to the situations that actually exist, area by area.

Under direction of USDA, training and more detailed guidance for farmers are being provided through the Agricultural Extension Service, including the County Agricultural Agents and Home Demonstration Agents.

RURAL WARNING

Because most farms are far from community centers and are often widely separated, warning that an attack is likely to occur, or has occurred in some part of the country, is a special problem. Even the most powerful sirens and horns would not have the necessary range. Many other warning systems have been suggested. They include use of partyline telephones (which are rapidly being replaced with more modern equipment); and systems of signal lights, or signal flags similar to those long used in coastal areas to warn of conditions likely to be dangerous to shipping and small craft. None of these, however, appears practical for general rural use. Conventional AM radio can give needed warning; but, of course, it is necessary to be within hearing of a receiver that is turned on. In periods of increased international tension, it is a good idea to keep a radio near, even taking a portable set into the fields during working periods.

THE FARM SHELTER

Many farm families live too far from population centers to make use of public shelters. Furthermore, they would need to care for poultry or livestock at the earliest time that it could be done without too great a personal exposure to radiation. Therefore, plans must be made to seek fallout protection on the farm. Such protection is available or can be improved in the same ways as were suggested in Chapter 5. However, there may be variations in type of construction and location of the shelter area to fit better the individual situations or needs. For example, existing structures such as a root cellar or storm cellar may be readily adaptable to use as fallout shelter (fig. 40). Where early care of livestock would be required, it would be well to have the shelter area close to or connected with the protected area for housing livestock. Most farms would be beyond the range of the immediate effects of nuclear explosions and could expect 30 minutes and usually longer before fallout would arrive. Therefore, a shelter area can be located a few hundred feet from the house, and the farmer and his family have ample time to reach safety. Guidance concerning types of shelter satisfactory for various farm needs is available from county agents. The requirements for providing emergency supplies, such as food and water, are the same as for other family shelter areas.

Many farms are so completely dependent upon electricity that even a brief loss of commercial power can cause serious problems. Therefore, an item of emergency equipment to be considered for both war emergency and natural disasters is a gasoline or diesel

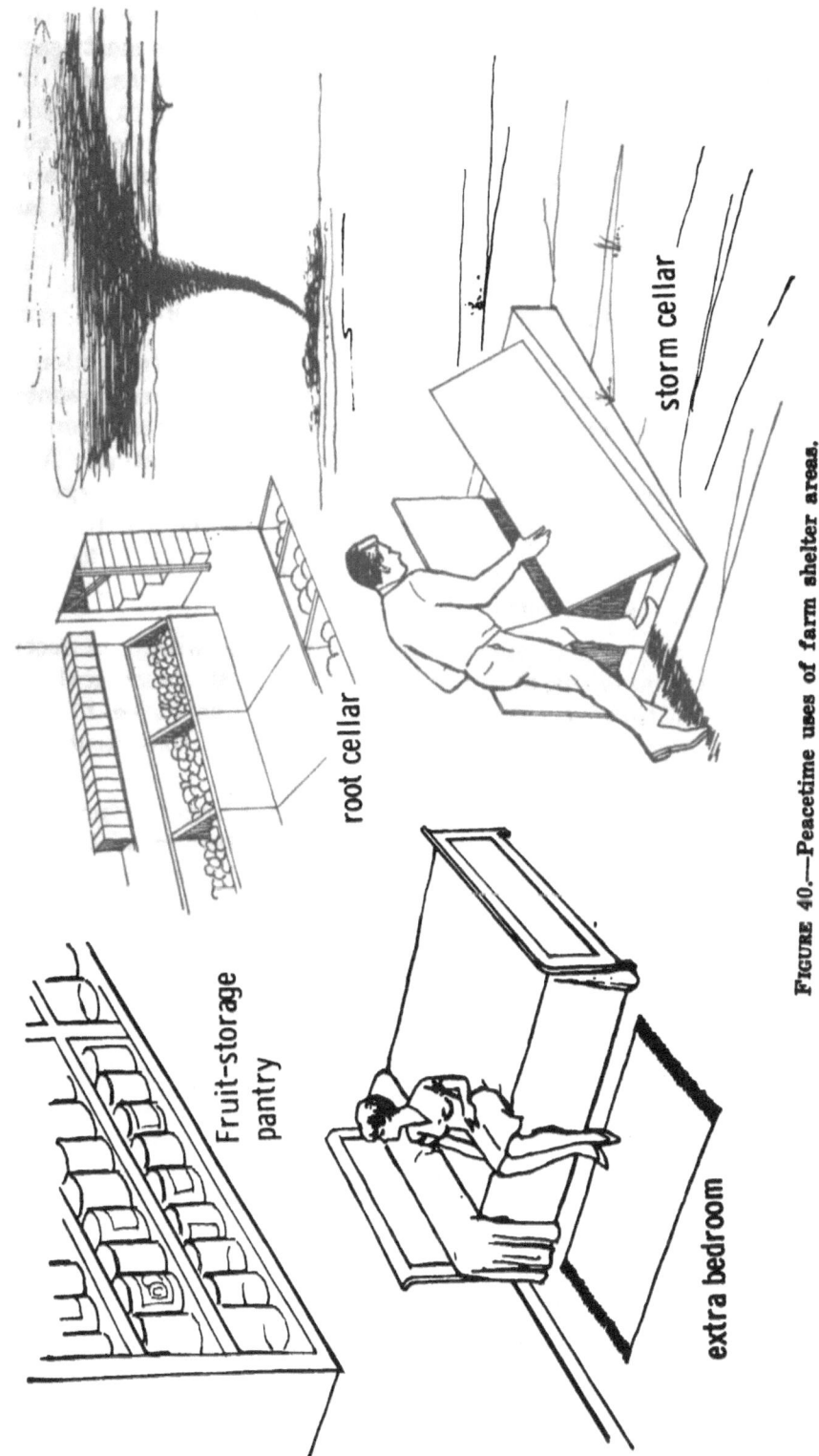

FIGURE 40.—Peacetime uses of farm shelter areas.

powered electric generator. It should supply 60-cycle alternating current at a voltage or voltages matching those of the most essential equipment. Its capacity must be adequate to handle the essential load. Such equipment might be located in a shielded compartment of the shelter, the exhaust being vented to the outside. Gasoline or diesel fuel storage should be at a safe distance outside the shelter, and its capacity should be great enough to last through the emergency period.

PROBLEMS OF FALLOUT ON THE FARM

The following section of this chapter is only an introduction to the solution of problems of fallout on the farm. They are presented for an understanding of what can be and what is being done to assure that food production will continue following attack. Also, for those farmers who have not yet prepared for an emergency, it can be a first step toward knowing how to prepare for such an event.

Radiation Exposure Control

As an emergency worker, the farmer must be willing to accept some risk in assuring that he will be able to continue agricultural production. However, his guiding principle should be to keep radiation exposures to the lowest practical limit consistent with saving community, family, and self.

During the first days and weeks in a fallout area, the principal hazard would be the gamma radiation from fallout. General information concerning the severity of the hazard could be expected by radio. However, radiation dose rates can vary a great deal over relatively short distances; and people will accumulate radiation doses at varying rates while performing tasks under varying degrees of protection. For these reasons, a farmer should own radiation measuring instruments so that he may check on his particular radiation hazards and keep track of his actual radiation exposure. Relatively inexpensive instruments suitable for these purposes are commercially available (see p. 29 for information on citizens radiological-monitoring instrument kits). The text on pages 24, 25 outlines the expected effects of various short-term whole-body doses of gamma radiation.

CARE OF LIVESTOCK AND POULTRY

Like man, animals are injured by both beta and gamma radiation, and where practicable should have protection. As with man, the gamma radiation would be a greater hazard than beta radiation. Figure 41 shows the dose of gamma radiation which would

FIGURE 41.—Median lethal radiation doses for representative livestock.

be fatal to 50 percent of the various animals shown if received within a single 3- or 4-day period.

Ideally, shelter should be provided for all of them. If time permits, it would be good practice to get herds and flocks under cover in barns or other structures. In some instances this may not be practicable. Where adequate fallout protection cannot be provided, heavy losses of flocks and herds can be expected in areas subjected to heavy fallout. A requirement to rebuild some herds from stock that could be protected or that were in less contaminated areas can be anticipated. Many existing farm structures provide some fallout protection. This protection can often be materially improved at nominal cost. Trench-type silos adapted for shelter use can provide good protection at relatively low cost, and can provide ready access to feed.

Livestock in barns and shelters must have food and water during the shelter period. Stored feed, hay, silage, grain, and concentrates should be quite free from fallout. Although well water would be preferable, thirsty livestock should be provided sufficient water to meet their needs, regardless of possible radioactivity.

Livestock left in the open—unprotected—would face three hazards: gamma radiation from the area around them; beta radiation from fallout particles sticking to their skins, or hides; and internal radiation from fallout on the grass they ate. In areas subjected to only moderate fallout, some or all of the livestock probably would survive. The effects of gamma radiation would be the controlling factor. Fortunately, only a fraction of the fallout from surface nuclear explosions over typical soil or rock could be expected to stick to foliage. Fallout is only partially soluble in water and most of the particles would soon sink to the bottom of a stream or pond, and the dissolved material would be greatly diluted. The hazard to animals from fallout taken into the body with foliage or water seems to be less serious than once thought. Some of the radioactive material of the ingested fallout is absorbed in the body and concentrated in bones or glands. Some appears in the milk of producing dairy cattle.

When radiation levels have decreased enough to permit care of unsheltered livestock, they should be supplied with uncontaminated feed (stored) if possible until wind, weather, and decay have removed most of the fallout from the grass or until new growth of grass overshadows the old.

FOOD FROM EXPOSED AND CONTAMINATED CROPS AND ANIMALS

Animals that have been in barn or shelter, and have had only stored feed and uncontaminated water, would be excellent sources of food. Meat, dairy, and poultry products should be wholesome, in the full sense of the word.

Apparently healthy animals that have been unprotected can still serve as sources of food as needed.

If needed for food during the emergency period, an animal could be slaughtered and used, since the meat would not be likely to contain concentrations of radioactive substances that would be dangerous to humans. The U.S. Department of Agriculture, Meat Inspection Division, has developed procedures to be used by its inspectors to assure wholesome supplies of meat.

Milk can be used as required to meet essential nutrition needs. If it is not required to be used immediately to sustain life, milk from cattle that have grazed on contaminated grass might be processed into cheese and other dairy products, and stored until its radioactivity has "decayed" to more acceptable levels. Crops ready for harvest at the time of attack might be lost to spoilage if local radiation levels were high enough to delay harvesting work. However, the majority of crops nearing maturity at the time of fallout arrival could be harvested and used. Normal food processing, peeling, threshing, washing, etc., will remove all or most of the fallout which might be present. In any case, studies indicate that the food and water contamination problem during the early postattack period is relatively minor compared to the problem of external exposure to fallout radiation. In the later postattack period, the hazard from ingested radioactive material may predominate.

Ample safe food stocks are available for use during the emergency period. In some areas, distribution of these stocks may be a temporary problem. In this case, a hungry or thirsty person or animal should not be denied food or water because of radioactive contamination. During the recovery period, precautions against long-term hazards such as strontium 90 will be taken as needed.

SUMMARY: SURVIVAL ON THE FARM

Survival on the farm—the survival of most farm families and agricultural production—can be achieved. Required are: fallout protection for farm families and livestock; application of farm safety procedures, including work schedules to control necessary exposures to radioactive fallout while caring for livestock; and an effective civil defense capability in local government, including radiological defense services and expert agricultural guidance.

APPENDIX

AN OUTLINE FOR FAMILY EMERGENCY PLANNING

The nearest public fallout shelter to our home is located at

The best route from our home to this shelter is

The location in our home that offers the greatest fallout protection is

Our Emergency Broadcast System (EBS) Station is

Its dial setting is ....

NAMES OF FAMILY MEMBERS				
Nearest shelter to work/school				
Best route planned?				
Is assistance to shelter needed?				
Who will provide?				
CD Training Completed:				
Personal and Family Survival				
Medical Self-Help				
Home Nursing				
First Aid				
Shelter Management				
Radiological Monitoring				
Firefighting				

NAMES OF FAMILY MEMBERS				
Family Responsibility for:				
Supplies to take to public shelter				
Home shelter area food				
Home shelter area water				
First aid and first aid supplies				
Eliminating fire hazards and firefighting				
Safe storage of vital family records				
Sanitation and sanitation supplies				
Maintenance of family shelter area				
Insure battery radio is available and working				

Special Personal Needs:

Serious allergies

Special medicines

Special foods

Infant Supplies ....

Checklist of supplies for family shelter area

........Water ....Battery radio
........Food ....Change of clothing
........Sanitation ....Citizens radiation meter
........First aid & medical ....Firefighting

Items we plan to take to public shelter:

www.ingramcontent.com/pod-product-compliance
Lightning Source LLC
Chambersburg PA
CBHW031120080526
44587CB00011B/1044